Closing *the* Teaching Gap

This book is dedicated to my father, John Henry Bartalo,
the greatest "natural teacher" I ever saw.

Closing *the* Teaching Gap

Coaching for Instructional Leaders

Donald B. Bartalo
Foreword by Grant Wiggins

CORWIN
A SAGE Company

CORWIN
A SAGE Company

FOR INFORMATION:

Corwin

A SAGE Company

2455 Teller Road

Thousand Oaks, California 91320

(800) 233-9936

Fax: (800) 417-2466

www.corwin.com

SAGE Ltd.

1 Oliver's Yard

55 City Road

London EC1Y 1SP

United Kingdom

SAGE India Pvt. Ltd.

B 1/I 1 Mohan Cooperative Industrial Area

Mathura Road, New Delhi 110 044

India

SAGE Asia-Pacific Pte. Ltd.

33 Pekin Street #02-01

Far East Square

Singapore 048763

Copyright © 2012 by Corwin

Printed in the United States of America

A catalog record of this book is available from the Library of Congress.

ISBN 978-1-4522-1709-3

This book is printed on acid-free paper

Acquisitions Editor: Arnis Burvikovs

Associate Editor: Desirée Bartlett

Editorial Assistant: Kimberly Greenberg

Production Editor: Amy Schroller

Copy Editor: Amy Rosenstein

Typesetter: C&M Digitals (P) Ltd.

Proofreader: Dennis W. Webb

Indexer: Jean Casalegno

Cover Designer: Rose Storey

Permissions Editor: Karen Ehrmann

12 13 14 15 16 10 9 8 7 6 5 4 3 2 1

Contents

Foreword

We all know the knock against education books and articles—nice ideas, but how practical is this? What can you *do* with it? Well, Don Bartalo has delivered: while built on a coherent framework of eight important reform tenets, the book is jam-packed with one good practical strategy after another for how to turn good ideas into effective and manageable action.

Nor are the practical ideas trivial or insufficiently detailed (as so often happens, even in books that aspire to be useful). He offers numerous useful tips on how to better manage time—a critical ability of school leaders. He describes in detail how key activities (such as Master Classes and developing a local belief system about learning) can be conducted for maximal ownership. And he grounds the advice and protocols in sophisticated ideas made accessible, such as his treatment of the theory-in-action work of Chris Argyris and colleagues.

As helpful and numerous as are the rich array of suggestions and their theoretical backing, Don has done something deeper here—something of signature importance in any book that aspires to be truly helpful: the book gives readers the courage to act. There is a can-do spirit that pervades the text; there is a no-nonsense optimism that led me to think—yes, *that's* do-able, *that* would work, even as a somewhat untested principal I could surely do *that*. In tone as well as in substance, therefore, this manual will enable readers to move forward with challenging reforms in the strong belief that change *is* possible.

By offering one useful action after another, by weaving in words of wisdom from veteran educators, by helping the reader see the link between concrete tips and overarching ideas and theory of action, by closing the book with one excellent and detailed success story after another, the book can perhaps best be summed up by an advertising slogan used by a large home-improvement chain a few years ago: you can do it; we can help.

No serious school leader should be without this book!

—Grant Wiggins
Understanding by Design, coauthor
Schooling by Design, coauthor

Preface

"It is somewhat surprising and discouraging how little attention has been paid to the intimate nature of teaching and school learning in the debates on education that have raged over the past decade."

—*The Culture of Education,*
Bruner, 1996 (p. 86)

This is a book for instructional leaders who want to learn more about how to help teachers improve their teaching methods. It is based on the belief and promise that if you become a better instructional leader, you will, in fact, be helping to close the teaching gap. The focus is on the fundamental nature of the instruction that occurs each day in the classroom. This book, by providing you with (a) new insights into leading instructional change, (b) ideas for helping teachers create better learning opportunities for students, (c) proven strategies for changing methods where students are not succeeding, (d) ways to improve results using a theory of action perspective, (e) leadership tools designed specifically for improving teaching, (f) approaches for developing shared instructional leadership, and (g) suggestions for enhancing self-improvement, will help you become a better instructional leader.

Yes, the education debates described by Bruner in 1996 are still raging today. These conversations, however, have been so taken up with noninstructional reform issues and policy changes that we have practically forgotten that "teaching is the activity most clearly responsible for learning" (Stigler & Hiebert, 2009, p. 3). Good teaching needs to be at the heart of any reform movement in the

United States. Expectations for increasing the level of student learning must be matched by efforts to improve teaching methods.

My understanding of good teaching comes from teachers like Mrs. Battaglia, my second-grade teacher, who had us kids thinking we were world explorers; from Miss Coonan, my fifth-grade teacher, who insisted that we question everything we studied; from Mr. Reeves, my seventh-grade social studies teacher, who had us debate the causes of the Civil War; and from Mr. Collins, my high school science teacher, who helped us discover physics applications at home and in school. Although the circumstances surrounding their work as teachers were certainly less complicated than today, there is a thread that runs so true for these teachers. They loved teaching, and they loved teaching their subjects. We need to return to this way of thinking and doing.

MY BELIEFS ABOUT
INSTRUCTIONAL LEADERSHIP

I have worked with many hundreds of students, teachers, and administrators in just about every way possible for an educator in public education. I have observed some exciting teaching and worked with education leaders dedicated to improving teaching and learning. They have taught me a great deal.

In recent years, however, I have seen teachers becoming increasingly frustrated. Even teachers recognized as highly effective say that they have lost some of the joy of teaching. These teachers tell me that their frustrations are mainly due to having to spend so much time preparing their students for tests. Has this been happening in your school or district?

As an instructional leadership developer and coach, I have listened to many administrators frustrated because they are not able to spend more time in classrooms. These administrators feel overwhelmed. Expanding leadership responsibilities and pressing accountability issues have taken them farther away from where they feel they belong—in classrooms.

I have seen the concept of instructional leadership rise out of a need to support and guide teachers asked to do more and more with students. Under the guise of needed school reform, these instructional leaders are asked to lead instruction in new directions with little or no support for their own growth and development. Because of this lack of instructional leadership support, throughout this book, I try to serve as your coach to help you enhance your leadership skills and develop effective strategies that you can feel comfortable using in your work to improve learning and teaching.

Good teaching, for example, can be observed. Instructional leaders need to hone their observational skills and make time to be in classrooms. They need to look at how teachers connect students with meaningful learning in ways that are interesting to students. Yes, caring for students is important, but caring is not enough. Teachers must know what to teach and how to teach it. Instructional leaders must know how to help teachers improve teaching. I believe this relationship of *learning and doing* forms the foundation of an effective instructional leadership practice. I feel strongly that this relationship has the potential to close the teaching gap described in Chapter 1.

The goal of good teaching is the same as the goal of good instructional leadership—to maximize learning for students and teachers. Accomplishing the goal has widespread meaning.

- For students, it means understanding what they are learning, connecting that understanding to new learning, and applying it in ways that are meaningful.
- For teachers, it means that they understand how students learn best and can translate that understanding into generating better learning opportunities for students.
- For instructional leaders, it means that they understand how to help teachers improve their practice and can turn that understanding into the action needed to lead desired instructional change.
- For parents, it means that they understand their role and how important it is to support the work of teachers, stay in close communication with the schools, and make sure their children are trying their best.
- For board members, it means that they understand their role as policymakers and turn that understanding into guidelines, procedures, and decisions that will strengthen and support student learning and effective teaching.

The goal to maximize student learning cannot be achieved unless more attention is paid to improving teaching methods. Oftentimes, classroom practice does not match what is known about how students learn best. This is the challenge that grounds this book in reality. The joy of teaching and learning, somewhat lost in the flood of school reform issues, can be reignited through the efforts of many, but especially through the efforts of a good instructional leader. Becoming that kind of instructional leader is what this book is about.

What Does It Take to Become a Better Instructional Leader?

This may sound a bit negative, but it is not easy to become a better instructional leader. There are many things that can go haywire, different personalities to satisfy, complicated account-ability issues to wrestle with, mushrooming initiatives, and many different beliefs about what constitutes effective teaching. The good news is that you can help yourself to improve. The bad news is that you will probably have to make some changes in the way you strive for improvement.

The work of an instructional leader crisscrosses the preferred teaching styles of many teachers and is set in the school's culture of teaching that does not come with a set of instructions. Inside this culture, you can find everything from the unrelenting quest to protect the status quo to the satisfaction that occurs when like-minded educators address student needs in ways that improve future learning.

EIGHT FUNDAMENTAL TENETS FOR AN INSTRUCTIONAL LEADER

Below are eight fundamental tenets that are essential for growth as an instructional leader. These eight tenets are the nuts and bolts of this book and are based on research tied to teaching and learning, experience, and common sense. Each one of these tenets will receive special attention in the chapters that follow. When viewed together, these eight tenets represent what an instructional leader must do in order to help teachers improve their teaching methods.

- *Develop an in-depth understanding of teaching and learning.* Nothing is more important for an instructional leader than understanding teaching and learning. This understanding should be based on how students learn best and helps to establish an instructional leader's credibility with teachers. It goes far beyond a simple knowledge of best practice. The need to better understand teaching and learning is one of the main reasons why good instructional leaders spend so much time observing in classrooms.

• *Maintain an insider's understanding of the school's culture of teaching.* Informed leadership is needed to address the challenges related to ongoing instructional improvement. Without an accurate picture of *workplace reality,* an instructional leader is as vulnerable as an ice fisherman on thin ice. Attempting to lead learning in a culture of teaching may include everything from having to deal with passive resistance to strengthening teamwork. An effective instructional leader must learn how to work within the culture of teaching that exists in the school. There is no guidebook for that.

• *Inspire teachers to create better learning opportunities for students.* Student learning depends in large measure on the quality of the learning opportunities students receive in classrooms. In order to inspire teachers to produce better learning opportunities for students, an instructional leader must make a personal investment in building relationships. This is leading by influence. Teachers are more apt to try to improve when they feel understood, trusted, and involved in the decisions that impact their teaching. A good instructional leader models the behavior and actions expected of others.

• *Work with teachers to change methods where students are not succeeding.* This is the toughest challenge for an instructional leader. Ironically, even when the need for a different teaching method is obvious to everyone involved, the agreed-upon instructional change may be perceived by some teachers as second-order in nature (i.e., beyond current competencies). This perception can easily become reality causing a desired instructional change to stall, fail, or end up on the shelf. A good instructional leader recognizes the critical relationship between how staff perceive desired change and the need to adjust leadership responsibilities and associated practices accordingly. Without a balance between perception and leadership response, the change will most likely fail.

• *Support teacher improvement.* Timing is everything. When teachers begin to move forward with their practice, they need to receive ongoing in-class support. Delivering on promised follow-up is another way for an instructional leader to earn credibility with teachers. This level of follow-up support includes a safe environment for teachers to take risks, coupled with timely and specific feedback aimed at reinforcing progress and overcoming barriers to success. Teacher-specific support is invitational, and the critical question from the instructional leader becomes: What do you want to learn next?

- *Help teachers learn more about teaching.* A professional acts on the most current knowledge that defines her field. The highest plane of professional development for teachers can be found in a culture of trust where teachers are in each other's classrooms learning about effective instruction from each other. But, for many teachers this is just too big a jump. Consequently, a good instructional leader looks for alternative ways to help teachers learn more about teaching. Collaborative analysis of student work is an example of one such way to promote this type of professional learning. Peer observations are treated like a series of approximations—one step at a time.

- *Understand the why behind the how.* The blend of principle and practice produces better teaching and stronger instructional leaders. That means having a working knowledge of student-centered research. An instructional leader needs to be able to explain why a certain method or proposed instructional change is worth considering. Developing a theory of action perspective (i.e., a way to move from the current to the desired state) gives teachers a better understanding of the why behind the how. A good instructional leader must be able to translate ideas into action (i.e., theory into practice).

- *Use self-reflection and staff feedback to improve.* Experiential learning is high on the list for self-improvement. An instructional leader can improve her practice by keeping a journal and seeking feedback from those who know her work the best. A reflective practitioner thinks about his work and is often able to make needed leadership adjustments based on earlier reflections. Although staff members may be hesitant to provide face-to-face honest feedback, a good instructional leader finds ways to help them do so.

CONNECTING YOUR WORK
AND EXPERIENCE

As I always say whenever I start a seminar with instructional leaders, "You did not come here today empty. You came here with front-line experience and knowledge that can be used to connect with new learning." It is what learning is all about—making connections. The same is true about reading this book. Build on your experience and use this opportunity to grow as an instructional leader.

No one needs to tell you that these are challenging times to be an instructional leader. You understand how important it is for you to help teachers give students the best learning opportunities possible. When that happens, students will learn more and you will feel the satisfaction of a job well done. But, you also know how frustrating it can be trying to improve teaching and learning.

The path to becoming a better instructional leader is not a simple one. It will require new thinking on your part and thoughtful action that might take you out of your comfort zone. This book is designed to help you do just that. Your degree of difficulty will be determined by how much you intend to learn and accomplish.

As you move through the book, allow your work experience to be your learning laboratory. You learn the most on the job, but sometimes it helps to have a steady frame of reference and a reason for self-reflection. I hope the ideas, suggestions, activities, tools, and strategies found in this book will guide and support your growth as an instructional leader.

Continuum of Instructional Leadership

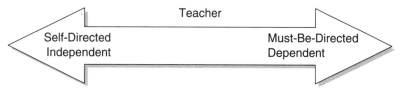

Most of us received better learning opportunities because a teacher decided that her teaching needed to improve. No one told her that she had to change. She changed because she knew that her teaching was not the best for students. This is the highest level

xviii CLOSING THE TEACHING GAP

of instructional leadership because it comes from the person most responsible for learning in the classroom—the teacher. Self-directed improvement is a wonderful thing to behold.

The same is true for principals who can pull a team of teachers together to develop an instructional program with project-based learning activities that truly excited students and helped them learn at higher levels. It happens when teachers and administrators center their work on improving instruction. This is also a wonderful thing to behold because it is the kind of instructional leadership that many teachers seem to need.

Unfortunately, too many classrooms have kids lined up row-by-row at their desks, listening to a boring lecture, when they should be actively involved in their learning. This is not a wonderful thing to behold. But, it represents one end of the continuum of instructional leadership (i.e., from self-directed to must-be-directed).

So what is my point? My point is that when there is a need to improve student learning, chances are there is also a need to improve instructional leadership. That need could be filled by teachers working alone, but often it requires the support and guidance of colleagues and good instructional leaders. Stigler and Hiebert (2009) point the way when they remind us that "the system must support teachers to improve teaching, because teachers are the key to closing the gap" (p. xx). One thing is for sure—students deserve great teaching.

ABOUT THE BOOK

I wrote this book because I believe that the results we are seeking in public education in the United States are only possible through good teaching. Look around your school. Ask yourself this question: Does the teaching match what we know about how students learn best? In the vast majority of situations, the answer to this question is easy to predict: "No." Our goal should be to be able to answer that question in the positive. Effective, dedicated instructional leaders can be important change agents to transform teaching and public education.

This book presents the actions needed to improve as an instructional leader. It serves as both a *what to do* and a *how to do it* resource. The contents are built on a solid foundation of research and my years of practical experience as an instructional leader, leadership developer, and coach.

The book is designed for principals, assistant principals, teachers developing as instructional leaders (e.g., grade and department chairs), assistant superintendents of instruction, and other school leaders with responsibility for improving teaching and learning. Written for practitioners like you, it assumes that the reader has some degree of background and experience in the field of instructional leadership. Together, we will build on that background and experience to help you become a better instructional leader.

As you go through the book, you may feel like you are being coached one-on-one, and in a way, you will be. The book contains the main responsibilities and tasks required of an instructional leader. So although face-to-face coaching is impossible, the book is written so you can reflect on your practice in ways that are similar to the coaching process. This interactive approach may provide the framework needed to help you dig deeper into your own growth as an instructional leader. Your insights into your work need to be tempered with reality. Just as there is no such thing as a perfect lesson, there is no such thing as a perfect instructional leader.

You will be able to use the book to not only help you validate current practice, but also to extend your thinking into new areas of development as an instructional leader. The book is designed to challenge your current thinking and actions. It does this by drawing you into a meta-cognitive exchange of learning and doing that personalizes the content around your particular job situation. If taken seriously, the book can help you to more quickly grasp what you need to understand and do in order to become more successful as an instructional leader. You will not be trying someone else's strategies; instead, you will be using the book to help you develop and plan your own strategies to improve the methods needed to close the teaching gap.

How the Book Is Organized

In each chapter of the book, you will find six common elements. Each element serves as a scaffold that supports a greater understanding of what is to come. The purpose of these scaffolding elements is to provide a more in-depth and focused inquiry into your work as an instructional leader. These elements are as follows:

- Springboards
- Voices of Experience
- Case Illustrations
- In-Your-Head Quizzes
- Research Moments
- Journal Reflections

Springboards

Springboards are carefully selected quotations found at the top of every chapter. The purpose for including these statements is to help you establish perspective. Point of view is essential to learning and is important for developing a deeper understanding of instructional leadership. After reading each quotation, take a few minutes to let the quotation sink in. Wrestle with its meaning for you. To illustrate the value of a Springboard, consider the quotation found at the beginning of the Introduction to this book.

"It is somewhat surprising and discouraging how little attention has been paid to the intimate nature of teaching and school learning in the debates on education that have raged over the past decade."—*The Culture of Education*, Bruner, 1996 (p. 86)

This statement speaks to a profound perspective about school improvement. The reader knows instantly that the person quoted believes that what is happening in the classroom is what is important to improving education. Yet for some strange reason, reform debates seldom mention the importance of improving the teaching methods. The reader begins to think about how much attention is being paid to improving the teaching methods in his own school situation. A point of view is re-examined and trumpets entry into the book.

Voices of Experience

It is often said that experience is a good teacher. In this book, you will have an opportunity to judge that saying for yourself. The book contains statements from five instructional leaders recognized for their ability to improve teaching and learning. Together they have more than 150 years of practical experience in rural, urban, and suburban school districts.

These five educators have been kind enough to share their thoughts about their efforts to become better instructional leaders. As a way of an introduction, below is a little background about each one of the Voices of Experience.

1. Ardis Tucker—Her 35 years of experience included employment as an instructional consultant, assistant superintendent for instruction, language arts director, reading teacher, teacher leader, and classroom teacher. Ardis worked primarily in rural and suburban schools. As an instructional leader, she worked to create classroom-learning environments that helped each student reach his/her potential.

2. Anita Clark—Her 33-year career includes work as an instructional leader and literacy consultant, principal, reading coach, teacher leader, and classroom teacher. Anita worked primarily in suburban and rural education. She considers herself an instructional leader because she worked with teachers to define what student learning should look like and identified instructional approaches that would support that learning.

3. Anthony Giannavola—During his 32-year career he has worked primarily in urban education in principal, assistant principal, and classroom teacher positions. As an instructional leader, Anthony constantly challenged teachers to improve their teaching proficiency in a mutually respective professional learning environment.

4. Jay Costanza—Jay has 30 years of experience as an instructional leader, adjunct professor, lead teacher, and classroom teacher. He has worked primarily in urban education. Jay considers himself an instructional leader because he has the ability to guide and coach both teachers and administrators in their efforts to better understand how students learn in order to improve student achievement schoolwide.

5. Bill Davis—Over his 32-year career, he has worked as an instructional leadership consultant, principal, and classroom teacher in primarily rural and suburban schools. In his role as an instructional leader, Bill has helped focus the nature of conversations and actions on student learning.

You will see their comments throughout the book in text boxes like the one featured below.

> "An instructional leader is a person who has the ability to learn, is a master teacher, and can engage in a reflective practice." ~ Anthony

These five instructional leaders do not pretend to be experts. They would each tell you how challenging it is to develop as an instructional leader. They are, in a sense, pioneers. They lived through the period in public education when school leaders went from being managers of a school to leaders of instruction. You cannot do that without learning quite a bit. As you read their comments, think about yourself and your own growth as an instructional leader. Use what they have to say to validate and rethink your own practices. I sometimes use collaborative reflections when I am coaching more than one person at a time or between myself and another leader. Let the "Voices of Experience" be your source of collaboration. Learn from them.

Case Illustrations

There are a number of Case Illustrations presented in the book. Case Illustrations are based on real problems of practice that have been accumulated over the years and are used to illustrate a particular point or concept. The reason for including Case Illustrations is to give you a pragmatic context for self-assessment using your own experience and leadership position as a frame of reference. The Case Illustrations are more for reflection than for teaching. The problems of practice are not meant to be case studies. As you go through a Case Illustration, visualize what you would do (or have done) in similar situations. Whenever possible, write down your responses to the reflection questions. Writing will help to clarify your thinking and consider other alternatives for the future.

In-Your-Head Quizzes

In-Your-Head Quizzes are like little personal challenges to give the reader an objective way to check understanding and the author an alternative way of making a lasting point. With all the testing going on these days it would be a shame not to include a few short-answer questions. The answer to this first one is, of course, instructional leader. The answers to the Quizzes appear on page 221. Good luck!

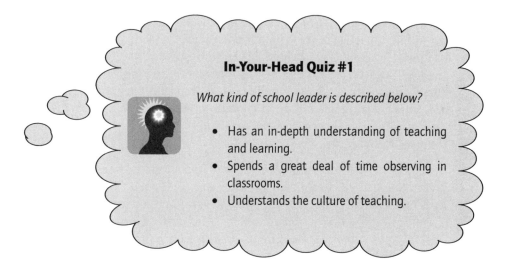

In-Your-Head Quiz #1

What kind of school leader is described below?

- Has an in-depth understanding of teaching and learning.
- Spends a great deal of time observing in classrooms.
- Understands the culture of teaching.

Research Moment

Leadership is second only to classroom instruction among all school-related factors that contribute to what students learn at school.
~ Leithwood, Seashore Lewis, Anderson, & Wahlstrom, 2004 (p. 3)

Each chapter has a Research Moment like the one above. It is a device to call your attention to an important piece of research linked to instructional leadership. Research Moments are single-focus reminders that research counts. Research tied to improving teaching and learning will help you substantiate your beliefs and actions as an instructional leader.

For example, the Research Moment from Leithwood and colleagues is significant because effective education leadership makes a difference in improving learning. There's nothing new or especially controversial about that idea. What's far less clear, even after several decades of school renewal efforts, is just how leadership matters, how important those effects are in promoting the learning of all children, and what the essential ingredients of successful leadership are.

The point here is that a good instructional leader must have a working knowledge of the educational research that grounds good teaching practice and related leadership responsibilities. Often teachers and other educators rely on an instructional leader's knowledge of research to help them make important instructional decisions. Keeping up-to-date with current research is a must.

 ### *Journal Reflections*

At the close of each chapter, you will find a Journal Reflection. It consists of three to four questions that are aligned to the content found in the chapter. The idea is to reinforce the importance of becoming a *reflective practitioner* as you relate what you have read to your own situation. The use of the term *reflective practitioner* is credited to Donald Schön (1983) when he theorized that "a reflective practitioner reflects on the phenomenon before him, and on the prior understandings which have been implicit in his behavior" (p. 68).

It is well known that professionals learn through action— through doing their jobs. Experience coupled with deliberate reflection on past performance, in a range of situations, can produce enriched understanding that guides instructional leadership growth and development. This deeper understanding fuels the notion of reflection-in-action and explains why some instructional leaders have the ability to not only think on their feet, but to see how they must work with teachers to design better learning opportunities for students. In this regard, reflection is futuristic.

It is a good practice to develop a weekly journaling habit. My advice for becoming a lifelong reflective practitioner is to find 15 minutes each week (e.g., before you go home on Friday afternoons) to write about your work. Include successes and as well as the challenges you face solving problems or making decisions. Returning to that journal every so often will give you a realistic idea of how you are developing as an instructional leader. It is an authentic form of self-assessment. Keep in mind the words of Vincent van Gogh (1887), who wrote in a letter to a friend that "reflection [makes] us see in ourselves."

LEARNING EXTENSIONS

At the end of each chapter, there are two learning extensions. These devices are designed to help you apply what you are thinking and learning directly into your work as an instructional leader. The first learning extension is for you as an individual and is called "Try THIS." This device is indicated by the icon shown below.

Try THIS are sidebar notes with tips, suggestions, and ideas for experienced and emerging instructional leaders. The following example should help you better understand how this personal learning extension will work in each chapter of the book.

You are beginning a book about instructional leadership where the book is like a coach. This is different from most books. Throughout the book, you will receive direct and indirect coaching about all facets of instructional leadership. This subconscious coaching, if you will, is real. It is based on years of experience coaching and working with instructional leaders from many different perspectives.

Take advantage of this opportunity to put yourself in a position to benefit from being coached. Be open to rethinking what you are doing and trying some things differently. Respond the way you would if your coach was sitting next you asking questions, giving you feedback, and providing ongoing support.

Try taking an action-oriented approach to reading this book.

The second learning extension is for you as a facilitator of a "Leadership Team Activity." There may be times when you are using the book with a leadership group and you might want some suggestions on how to facilitate a particular aspect of the book or a group-learning process. This learning extension device helps to maximize the use of the book and is indicated by the icon shown below.

The example found in the shaded box below should help you better understand how this facilitator extension will work in each chapter of the book. It will serve as a guide as you apply or extend knowledge with an instructional leadership team. The format is flexible (you may wish to modify the process), but is structured in ways that will increase group participation and collective leadership learning in about a 60-minute single-focus seminar setting. The purpose of this extension is always to build on thinking and learning generated by the book.

 LEADERSHIP TEAM ACTIVITY

Orientation to Learning Together

Purpose

Start with the end in mind.

- Understand how valuable it is for a team of instructional leaders to explore a topic or concept together.
- Visualize the action needed to transfer seminar learning and understanding to current instructional leadership practice.

Perspective

- A lot has been written about the value of professional learning communities. Regrettably, there is little evidence that this concept has progressed beyond collegial relationships.

Challenge

- To be effective, an instructional leader must be able to put good intentions into thoughtful actions that will improve teaching and learning.

Plan

- The basic steps for facilitating a tailor-made seminar (1 -2 -3).

Personal and Team Connections

- Participants will be asked to connect their unique leadership challenges to the content of the seminar.
- The team will ask two essential questions: (1) What have we been learning? (2) How can we use this learning to strengthen our work as instructional leaders?

This is my first book, but not, as the phrase goes, my first rodeo. My experience as an educator transcends everything from filmstrip projectors to SMART boards, from open education to programmed learning, and from do your own thing to mandated standardization. Take the opportunity this book affords to revive yourself as an instructional leader. Come to terms with what you really believe is the way students learn best. Base those beliefs on classroom observations and solid research and use those beliefs to guide your work with teachers. As you grow as an instructional leader, you will gain confidence in knowing that you are closing the teaching gap by helping teachers to improve their teaching methods.

Acknowledgments

First, and foremost, I am indebted to all of the wonderful teachers, principals, and assistant principals whom I have worked with over my career. They each had a part in building my understanding of instructional leadership, coaching, and what it takes to create better learning opportunities for students.

I am especially indebted to Jay Costanza, Anita Clark, Bill Davis, Anthony Giannavola, and Ardis Tucker, the five instructional leaders who are featured in the book as the "Voices of Experience." They were indeed pioneers of effective instructional leadership.

I am indebted for the assistance I received from the Corwin team: Arnis Burvikovs, Desirée Bartlett, Kimberly Greenberg, Amy Schroller, Amy Rosenstein, Rose Storey, and Karen Ehrmann. They helped a first-time author find his way. Special thanks to Debbie Stack for her excellent first-draft editing and suggestions on writing style.

I also want to thank my good friend and fellow Corwin author, Doug Llewellyn, for his advice and suggestions as the book neared completion. Thanks also to my son Brian, a high school principal, and my daughter Kristin, an arts integration specialist, who always found time to talk "shop" with their father.

Finally, a special word of appreciation to my wife Denise, a literacy specialist and outstanding teacher, for her tremendous support and understanding not only during the writing of this book, but during all of the years my travel took me away from home.

Publisher's Acknowledgments

Corwin would like to thank the following individuals for graciously providing their editorial insight and guidance:

Laurie Emery, Principal

Old Vail Middle School

Vail, Arizona

Lisa Graham, Program Specialist

Curriculum & Staff Development

Vallejo City Unified School District

Vallejo, California

Linda Jungwirth, President

Convening Conversations, Inc.

Faculty, Pepperdine University

Redlands, California

Elizabeth J. Lolli, Superintendent

Monroe Local School District

Monroe, Ohio

Wanda Mangum, Language Arts Instructional Coach

Curriculum and Instruction Department

Gwinnett County Public School District

Suwanee, Georgia

Bonnie Tryon, Principal for Instructional Planning
    and Support (Retired)

Cobleskill-Richmondville Central School

Cobleskill, New York

Marianne R. Young, Principal

Monument Mountain Regional High School

Great Barrington, Massachusetts

About the Author

 **Donald B. Bartalo** is a nationally recognized instructional leadership developer and coach with K–12 experience as a teacher, teacher leader, assistant principal, principal, and superintendent of schools. He has worked in rural, suburban, and urban school districts across the country and in his home city.

Donald is the head of his own consulting company, UNITY Instructional Leadership Development and Coaching, with a mission to support school leaders helping teachers to create better learning opportunities for students.

Still practicing as an instructional leadership developer and coach, Donald's unique ability is to help educators become better instructional leaders. Coaching is at the core of his education leadership.

Donald is a strong advocate for just and meaningful education and is an activist for improving the conditions of learning for students and teachers. He is a member of the national Save Our Schools Steering Committee.

Donald and his wife, Denise, live in Rochester, New York, and are the proud grandparents of four grandchildren.

BRIDGE TO CHAPTER 1

This book has been designed to be your coach. If you take an active role as a reader and respond to the many invitations to apply new thinking and learning to your work, it will help you to use proven instructional leadership methods and strategies to improve teaching and learning. The challenges you face as an experienced or as an emerging instructional leader with responsibilities for raising academic achievement during a time of unprecedented accountability demand your full attention. Let the book help prepare you as a highly effective instructional leader.

Since this book is about improving instructional leadership and closing the teaching gap, it is essential that the reader understands what is meant by the *teaching gap*. The purpose of Chapter 1 is to define the teaching gap and to explain how closing the teaching gap parallels the path to becoming a better instructional leader. The idea of a teaching gap was first introduced by Stigler and Hiebert (1999), and so it is important to make sure that the reader has at least a working knowledge of their research findings and principles of improvement. What follows is a summary of Stigler and Hiebert's conclusions about improving teaching together with some direct implications for instructional leaders.

CHAPTER ONE

The "Teaching Gap"

"The teaching gap we describe refers to the differences between the kinds of teaching needed to achieve the educational dreams of the American people and the kind of teaching found in most American schools. Although many of the American teachers we observed were highly competent at implementing American teaching methods, the methods themselves were severely limited.

The teaching gap becomes even more significant when one realizes that while other countries are continually improving their teaching approaches, the United States has no system for improving. The United States is always reforming but not always improving. The most alarming aspect of classroom teaching in the United States is not how we are teaching now but that we have no mechanism for getting better. Without such a mechanism, the teaching gap will continue to grow."

—*The Teaching Gap*, Stigler and Hiebert,
2009 (pp. xviii–xix)

WHAT IS THE TEACHING GAP?

The Teaching Gap, by James W. Stigler and James Hiebert (1999, updated in 2009), is based on a comparative analysis of two international studies of teaching (Third International Mathematics and Science Study—TIMSS). Although they studied mathematics teaching, the research of Stigler and Hiebert (1999) was selected to anchor this book because it represents the most in-depth look at teaching ever assembled. For this reason, the findings of Stigler and Hiebert (1999) have direct application for improving the teaching methods in any subject area. The major findings from their first comprehensive video study of classroom teaching in Japan, Germany, and the United States, summarized below, have implications for instructional leaders.

Finding #1:   Teaching, Not Teachers, Is the Critical Factor (pp. 10–11). Americans tend to focus on factors of competence (e.g., more rigorous certification process) rather than the methods used by teachers in the classroom. Even the best teachers, the ones judged the most competent, cannot be effective if the methods they are using do not promote better student learning. Put simply, it is what teachers say and do in the classroom that makes the difference in learning. For example, teaching methods include the decisions and choices teachers make when establishing the role of the students, how students solve problems, asking questions, explaining concepts, assigning homework, lecturing, teaching mini-lessons, giving demonstrations, setting up learning experiences and activities, and facilitating projects. The methods used greatly impact results. This finding is significant for an instructional leader to understand because there is a great need to help teachers learn more about teaching from their own experience and work in the classroom. The challenge for you as an instructional leader is to learn how to help teachers learn more about teaching—traditional professional development will not do it. "By seeing teacher learning as necessarily tied to the study of teaching, U.S. educators can begin to change the culture of teacher training" (Stigler & Hiebert, 2009, p. 33).

Finding #2:   Teaching Is a Cultural Activity (pp. 11–12). The international video studies revealed that while teaching methods vary greatly from country to country, the teaching methods used by teachers in the same country are very similar. Stigler and Hiebert learned that much of what happens in the classroom is determined by what they called the "DNA of teaching." The teaching methods are handed down from generation to generation through a *cultural code* that is present in most classrooms. This code is the main reason why changing teachers does not automatically produce changes in teaching. This finding is noteworthy for an instructional leader because improving teaching is not done in a vacuum—it is done as part of a culture of teaching that is complex and often difficult to influence. Recognizing the cultural nature of teaching can be a great help to the success of an instructional leader because it is the same culture that surrounds teacher learning.

Finding #3: A Gap in Methods for Improving Teaching (pp. 12–13). Stigler and Hiebert (1999) discovered that while American teachers have been trying their best to implement reform measures and recommendations, there is little evidence that the teaching has substantively changed. The changes they reported from the most recent TIMSS video study were described as superficial and having no profound impact on the way students learned. Stigler and Hiebert (1999) argue that if the United States is serious about improving student learning, then there must be a classroom-based system put into place to improve teaching methods. They proposed using a system of lesson study (explained in Chapter 4), which makes it possible for teachers to learn together about what constitutes effective teaching and to share that knowledge with other educators. This finding is important for an instructional leader to understand because you are in the best position to help teachers learn more about teaching and to put this goal into motion. Stigler and Hiebert warn that improving teaching is not a matter of designing new policy initiatives—we have tried that unsuccessfully. The real work of improving teaching must come from the teacher's own learning. Empower teachers to be more self-directed.

LESSONS FROM THE TEACHING GAP

The relationship of the teaching gap to becoming a better instructional leader is based on trying to solve the problem of how to improve teaching. Stigler and Hiebert (2009) call for a wide-scale plan that will systematically improve teaching and lead to more effective methods used in American classrooms. Although similar in terms of desired outcome (i.e., improved student learning), the perspective of an instructional leader trying to solve this complicated problem is slightly different from that of an educational researcher. An instructional leader, as Stigler and

Hiebert (2009) have acknowledged in their work, is faced with the daunting task of solving the improvement problem while teachers and students are walking in and out of classrooms every day. This is the challenge an instructional leader faces trying to improve teaching. It is the contention in this book that lessons learned from recognizing the teaching gap can help instructional leaders improve teaching and maximize learning.

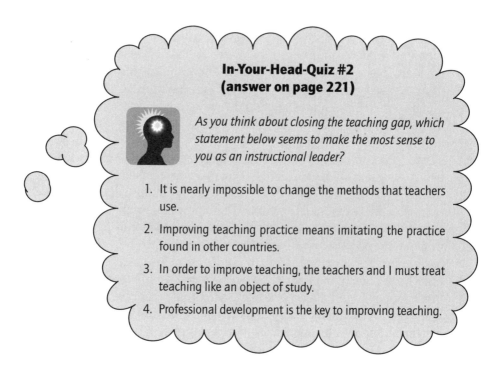

In-Your-Head-Quiz #2 (answer on page 221)

As you think about closing the teaching gap, which statement below seems to make the most sense to you as an instructional leader?

1. It is nearly impossible to change the methods that teachers use.
2. Improving teaching practice means imitating the practice found in other countries.
3. In order to improve teaching, the teachers and I must treat teaching like an object of study.
4. Professional development is the key to improving teaching.

In 1999, Stigler and Hiebert set the stage for improving teaching across the United States by proposing six principles for what they called "gradual, measurable improvement" (p. 131). Because these six principles are closely related to the goal of this book, which is to improve instructional leadership, they will be presented here so those connections can be reinforced. Keep in mind that Stigler and Hiebert believe that a method of collaborative lesson study (described in Chapter 4) is one process for improving teaching that is fully consistent with these six principles. For the purposes of this book, each principle will be reviewed from the point of view of an instructional leader.

Principle #1: Expect Improvement to Be Continual, Gradual, and Incremental (Stigler & Hiebert, 1999, p. 132). Because teaching is embedded in a "surrounding culture" of the school, you cannot expect to make great changes overnight. As a developing instructional leader, you know that this principle has merit. You have probably seen many instructional initiatives come and go with little or no capacity developed at the point of delivery—namely, the day-to-day practice of teachers in classrooms. As Americans, we are not noted for our patience and often exhibit a fast-food delivery mentality for just about everything, including the education of our students. Efforts to improve teaching methods will be realized slowly, but if done the right way, those changes will be significant for student learning over time.

Principle #2: Maintain a Constant Focus on Student Learning Goals (Stigler & Hiebert, 1999, pp. 132–133). The purpose of good teaching is good learning. As an instructional leader, you have no doubt felt the impact of this principle, especially over the past 10 years. But, with all the pressure to reform schools and improve student achievement, the details of implementing new programs and systems (e.g., the flurry of data-based decision-making) often blur the vision of learning. Learning improves when what is taught becomes more interesting to students. The challenge for an instructional leader is to help teachers develop learning opportunities that not only improve student learning, but that motivate students to want to learn. We know how to increase test scores, but an instructional leader must also know how to help teachers increase their knowledge of teaching. When this happens, teaching methods improve.

Principle #3: Focus on Teaching, Not Teachers (Stigler & Hiebert, 1999, pp. 133–134). One of the most intriguing aspects of the Stigler and Hiebert research is what they call "scripts for teaching" (p. 87). A cultural script, the authors argue, are mental versions of teaching patterns that all of us learn while we go through school. These patterns are widely shared by teachers and may account for similarities in teaching roles so common throughout a particular culture. For example, a pattern found in many U.S. classrooms is the teacher going over homework before teaching the heart of a lesson.

Because teachers have the same mental scripts, it is easy to predict patterns in their lessons. Here is the point from all of this: Teacher effectiveness depends on the scripts teachers use. An instructional leader, like a teacher addressing students' misconceptions at the start of a lesson, must not only be aware of embedded patterns of teaching, but understand how these patterns can interfere with attempts to modify teaching methods even when teachers are willing to do so.

It bears repeating. The problem in the United States is that we have put the emphasis on improving the competency of teachers rather than on improving the teaching methods used by competent teachers. Instructional leaders, while still interested in recruiting and maintaining good teachers, must align their work with the development of effective teaching methods. This means, among other things, helping teachers to rethink the decisions and choices they make when teaching. Think of it this way—if you can improve the methods that good teachers use, you will have achieved improvement that lasts.

Principle #4: Make Improvements in Context (Stigler & Hiebert, 1999, pp. 134–135). As an instructional leader, you have seen this principle in action as more and more school improvement plans are focusing on classroom-based learning for teachers. The emergence of the concept of professional learning communities is testimony to the impact of this principle, but unfortunately, just learning how to work together is not enough. The context for making improvements is complex and includes the teachers, students, curriculum, grouping, scheduling, and resources. All of these elements, and others that impact the classroom, must be considered when trying to improve teaching methods. One-shot attempts at implementing best practices fail because school-based essentials are not taken into account. If it were possible to just borrow innovation from high-performing countries, we would have probably done it by now, but we have not (nor should we).

Stigler and Hiebert (2009) contend that American educators understand the importance of context when it comes to student learning, but not so much when it comes to teacher learning. Too much of teacher learning, despite years of rhetoric about teachers learning in classrooms, is still focused on implementing programs or making data-based decisions rather than improving teaching methods. Even when instructional programs change (e.g., moving toward conceptual mathematics), often the teaching methods do not. The results fall short of expectations because the same methods are used, but in different ways with different learning materials. As an instructional leader, you understand the importance of teachers learning together, but you must also understand what they are learning and how this influences the decisions and choices they make while teaching. This book is devoted to helping you learn how to make the classroom the basis for teacher learning, and in so doing, help teachers create better learning opportunities for students.

Principle #5: Make Improvement the Work of Teachers (Stigler & Hiebert, 1999, pp. 135–136). Teachers have always been responsible for student learning, but have they shouldered the same level of responsibility for teacher learning? This is a question that every instructional leader needs to think about, because in the end, only teachers can provide the solutions to the problem of improving teaching methods. Will teachers need additional support in order to learn more about teaching? Of course, but that support cannot remove teachers as the "primary force behind change." Why is this belief so important for an instructional leader to understand? Teachers are the closest to the learning, and like doctors and nurses with health care, are in the best position to be able to carry out what is needed to improve student learning. A premise of this book is that instructional leaders, using appropriate levels of support and guidance, can lead the way by entrusting instructional change to teachers—those closest to the learning. Teachers are the solution to the problem of improving teaching, and instructional leaders are the solution to helping teachers make those improvements. In short, if it is not happening in the classroom, it is not happening.

Principle #6: Build a System That Can Learn From Its Own Experience (Stigler & Hiebert, 1999, pp. 136–137). Stigler and Hiebert imagine a system that allows U.S. educators to "harvest" what good teachers are learning about teaching and to share what they have learned so others can try these new approaches. It is a system that some other countries have in place (e.g., Japan and Finland), which supports "teachers developing their own knowledge of what works and what doesn't work in their own classrooms" (p. 136). For an instructional leader, this principle means that teachers working together in a school to improve teaching methods should have a way of keeping track of what they are learning and a means for sharing that learning with colleagues. The teaching methods that are being developed need to see the light of day and become the focal point for collaboration and study. This is a place where instructional leaders can really help by developing ways to build a knowledge base of improved teaching methods (e.g., recorded teaching episodes).

The foundations and principles put forth by Stigler and Hiebert (1999, 2009) should be used by instructional leaders to rethink the strategies needed to help teachers improve teaching. But, one lesson seems to stands out among all the rest. Unless the culture of teacher learning (i.e., how teachers learn to improve teaching methods) in the United States is changed, higher levels of student learning will continue to lag behind expectations. The research below provides a graphic representation of why there is a need to change the way we approach teacher-led instructional improvement in the United States.

Improving Instruction

Figure 1.1   Teachers' Activities to Improve Instruction

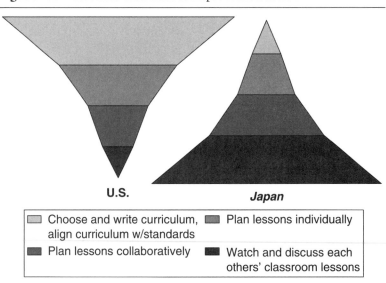

Reprinted with permission from Catherine C. Lewis. (2002). *Lesson Study. A Handbook for Teacher-led Instructional Improvement.*

Figure 1.1 clearly shows a major difference between how U.S. and Japanese teachers work to improve teaching. It dramatically reinforces the findings and principles put forth by Stigler and Hiebert and provides evidence that "improving teaching cannot succeed without changes in the culture of teacher learning" (1999; *Kappan*, November 2009, p. 32). But, this does not mean that U.S. educators can simply imitate the work with teacher-led instructional improvement being done in Japan. It does mean, however, that U.S. educators can learn from Japanese experience and that there is a definite need to rethink our systems for improving teaching. Instructional leaders are often in the best position to help teachers learn how to learn about teaching.

REINFORCING THE NEED TO CLOSE THE TEACHING GAP

The Organization for Economic Co-operation and Development (OECD) published a report titled *Strong Performers and Successful Reformers in Education: Lessons from the Program for International Student Assessment (PISA) for the United States* (2010). The testing measured the ability of 15-year-olds (near the end of compulsory education) to use the domains of reading, mathematical, and scientific literacy, not merely in terms of mastery of the school curriculum, but in terms of important knowledge and skills needed in adult life. Tests were administered to between 4,500 and 10,000 students in each country. The comparative results did not take into account measures of poverty.

Below are some key points from the 2009 OECD report that mirror and reinforce the research findings of Stigler and Hiebert. These points reflect teacher practices in countries that ranked at the top of the study and provide food for thought for American educators.

- Teachers are expected to contribute to the knowledge base on effective teaching practices.
- Teachers are involved in a collaborative process of lesson development and work together in a disciplined way to improve the quality of the lessons they teach.
- Improved instructional practice is institutionalized and often examples of effective teaching are videotaped and used as models for other teachers to learn from.

- No teacher's classroom is private, and teachers often observe the practice of colleagues.
- Teachers would not think of themselves as professionals if they did not carefully study the most effective methods for increasing student learning.

You can see from this list that teaching is indeed a cultural activity. This book is not about duplicating conditions that exist in other countries. This book is about whether or not you believe there is a need to improve the teaching methods used in your school. If you believe that there is a teaching gap in your school, then this book will help you to address that gap and improve student learning.

Some examples of possible gaps in teaching are listed below:

Teaching that does not recognize and address inaccurate and insufficient prior knowledge (e.g., misconceptions about concepts and ideas).

Teaching that does not produce opportunities for students to learn how to organize knowledge.

Teaching that does not construct opportunities for students to practice integrating skills and to understand when and how to apply them.

Teaching that does not give students constructive targeted feedback that enhances the quality of their learning.

Teaching that does not help student to make connections between new learning and what they already know.

Teaching that does not help students to become self-directed learners with the ability to monitor and adjust their approaches to learning.

Teaching that does not generate opportunities for students to be actively involved in their learning.

Teaching that does not help students connect facts with major concepts, big ideas, and general principles for a deeper understanding.

Teaching that does not involve students in the planning of what they will be doing to learn.

Teaching that does not develop opportunities for students to see the relevance in what they are learning.

Teaching that does not create opportunities for students to question what they are learning, relate new ideas to old ones, and apply an idea to a real problem.

Teaching that does not design opportunities for students to see the value of their work and learning.

Teaching that does not provide opportunities for students to develop deeper understanding on their own.

"To *learn* how to improve teaching requires teachers to leave their classrooms to dialogue with colleagues about best practice; to share what is working and what is not working with colleagues; to observe best practice in other classrooms; to be a part of a working professional learning community."
~ Bill

JOURNAL REFLECTION

Take time to write in your journal. Here are some suggestions for possible topics and subtopics to write about. Select the one that you believe will provide the greatest insights into your work now.

Big Picture

Think about how teachers in your school learn how to improve their teaching methods.

- What do you believe needs to change in order for teachers to improve teaching?
- What can you do to guide and support that change?

Experience

Think of a time when you were working with teachers to improve teaching methods. This does not mean implementing a new program, but rather, fundamentally changing how instruction is delivered in the classroom (e.g., allowing students more time to struggle with problem-solving or concept development).

- What did you do as an instructional leader to support the teachers' efforts to improve their teaching?
- What did you learn from this experience that will help you to improve teaching methods in the future?

Future

Where do you see the greatest need to bridge the teaching gap in your school? What can you do to begin closing that gap?

TRY THIS: GAP ANALYSIS

The idea of a teaching gap set forth in Chapter 1 is not meant to be a negative statement about teachers or teaching. Professionals often feel they must adjust their practice in accordance with prevailing conditions.

The era of accountability with high-stakes testing that was ignited in the 1980s has been just such a condition in education. Slowly but surely, many teachers began to back away from preferred student-centered methods in favor of methods that would produce better test results.

At the elementary level, it was the way the teaching of reading vacillated between basal reader and literature-based approaches. At the secondary level, it was the rapid decline of project-based learning.

So . . . try THIS:

- In order to bring the teaching gap to the conscious level with staff, pull together a group of six to eight teachers that you believe are highly effective—the best of the best.
- Provide a comfortable setting with light refreshments and a zero threat of a subjective atmosphere (risk free).
- Give everyone a copy of the Chapter 1 Springboard quotation from Stigler and Hiebert (2009) (p. 1). Ask the teachers to think about their own teaching with respect to this statement. Encourage the teachers to be as candid as possible.
- Reflect on what you learn.

LEADERSHIP TEAM ACTIVITY

Five Principles to Strengthen Instructional Leadership.

Purpose

Start with the end in mind.

- To build capacity for achieving realistic expectations about instructional improvement and overall effectiveness in grade levels and departments.
- Visualize the action needed to transfer seminar learning and understanding to current instructional leadership practice.

Perspective

- There has to be a realistic understanding of improvement that is shared by administrators, teacher leaders, and teachers. Too often there is a feeling conveyed from the top down that improvement needs to happen overnight. Stigler and Hiebert provide five important principles to guide expectations about school improvement.

Challenge

- To be effective, an instructional leader must work closely with teacher leaders so there is a clear understanding of what is meant by school improvement. This understanding may not always coincide with district, board, or community wishes.

Plan

The basic steps for facilitating this single-focus seminar:

1. Provide time for a 60-minute seminar with a team of grade or department chairs.
2. Go through each of the *first* Five Principles for Gradual, Measurable Improvement (found on pp. 5–7).
3. Use the following questions to guide the discussion: (a) What does each principle mean to the team? (b) How has your school and grade level or department been doing with each principle? (c) What is some evidence of gradual, measurable improvement?

(Continued)

(Continued)

Personal and Team Connections

- Participants will be asked to connect their unique leadership challenges to the content of the seminar.
- The leadership team will ask two essential questions: (1) What have we been learning? (2) How can we use this learning to strengthen our work as instructional leaders?

BRIDGE TO CHAPTER 2

You might be thinking this all sounds good, but where will I find the time? Look no further, because you are probably already spending most of your time, often unconsciously, trying to improve student learning. What is being suggested in this book will not give you more time, but it will help you to refocus your instructional leadership efforts on improving teaching methods that will result in increased student learning.

The recognition of a gap in teaching is a sign that the profession we call education is in need of some adjustments for the future. The Race to the Top (U.S. Department of Education, 2009) will not be won by incentives, competitive grants, or corporate rewards; it will be "won" (if that is the proper way to say it) by improving the teaching in classrooms. The conditions for improving teaching in the United States are, unfortunately, not yet in place. However, for now, you are being asked to look more closely at the conditions that affect your work as an instructional leader. It is the starting point for self-improvement.

Do you know if you are doing the right things? It is easier to tell when you are doing the wrong things. The next chapter may help you answer this question because it zeroes in on some important aspects of being an instructional leader, especially ways to improve your organizational management so you have more time to spend on instructional matters. These *habits of practice* will help you to understand where you may need to eliminate or reduce activities that do not contribute to your overall effectiveness as an instructional leader and your ability to help teachers improve their teaching methods.

CHAPTER TWO

Doing the Right Things

"Leaders are not being paid for knowing. They are being paid for getting the right things done."

—Peter Drucker, 2006 (p. xiii)

DATA INFORMED, NOT DATA DRIVEN

The most important information for a teacher does not come from a printout of a state test, but from observing students, looking at their work, and talking with them. Good teachers view observations as formative assessments. These teachers use what they are learning directly from students to inform instruction and guide decision-making. The same is true for a good instructional leader. Her work with teachers is based on multiple sources of evidence of student learning. Standardized tests are just one part of that evidence. A data-informed instructional leader can help teachers pinpoint student needs and solve complex instructional problems.

One way to facilitate a data-informed process is to have teachers look at student work together. For example, a team of fifth-grade teachers interested in improving nonfiction writing looked at a few short essays written by their students about weather prediction (the data). The teachers all had copies of the writing samples and went

15

through each one of them together. The value of teachers looking at student work together is of course the analysis. Often teachers find collaborative analysis the most challenging aspect of this process. To help the teachers with the analysis, the instructional leader asked the teachers to answer three questions about each piece of writing:

1. What do these students know about weather prediction?

2. What challenges are they facing trying to write about weather predictions?

3. What should our next teaching points be?

As the teachers went through each student's writing, they recorded the answers to these three questions on chart paper. After looking at four or five short essays, the teachers began to see some areas that needed to be addressed in their teaching. One glaring need was to help students better understand the difference between narrative and nonfiction writing. The students were also having difficulty putting the information they were learning about weather prediction into their own words. Near the end of the session, the teachers outlined several possible teaching points for follow-up lessons.

DEVELOPING CREDIBILITY

One of the catch phrases in education in the first decade of the 21st century is "capacity building." It just seems like everyone wants to build capacity for one thing or another. For an instructional leader, a capacity you need to build is credibility. Credibility means that the teachers believe you know what you are talking about (competency) and that you will be true to your word (consistency). One way to earn credibility with teachers and other staff members is by following through on what you said you were going to do.

How do you feel when someone tells you they are going to do something, and then they either never do it or they do not get around to doing it for a long time? Follow-through is something that does not cost a cent, but it can make a big difference between success and mounting frustration. Teachers become frustrated when their instructional leaders (peer or administrative) make promises they do not keep. With so many instructional improvement initiatives underway in most schools these days, it is understandable how things can be backed up. Unless you are in a position to limit projects, however, you have no choice but to make sure you follow-through on the ones underway. Your personal involvement and presence cannot be delegated. Principals and assistant principals have to be careful about leading from the office.

> "Be involved in the same professional development as teachers so that everyone grows together and speaks the same language." ~ Jay

FINDING STRENGTHS IN OTHERS

Here is a mental example for you to try. Think of five of the best teachers you work with. Jot their initials down. Now, next to each set of initials, write down a strength you have seen in the person that they may not be recognizing. For example, one of the teachers may be skilled at analyzing reading records to inform teaching. Think about how you could help these five teachers to recognize their unique abilities to enrich their professional lives. For instance, a teacher who develops highly interactive lessons may be willing to share her ideas at a professional conference.

When you look for teacher strengths, you are setting an example. You are reminding and modeling for the teachers how important it is for them to do the same with their students. Too often it is the other way around, and student weaknesses get all the attention. The way forward for all learners, students, and teachers is through their strengths. Now the idea here is not to get hokey. Artificial recognition is worse than none. Finding strengths in others has to be legitimate and, most importantly, it has to be handled carefully. For example, broadcasting a teacher's strengths at a faculty meeting has to be done in ways that will not make others in the room feel that their accomplishments are being overlooked.

"Help teachers recognize their own strengths while at the same time pushing them to stretch their thinking and skills." ~ Bill

GETTING INTO CLASSROOMS

Look at your calendar for the past 3 weeks (15 days). How many of those days did you make at least one classroom visit for at least 20 minutes? If your numbers are low, you may need to take some corrective action. Glickman (2002) has it right when he says, "In the most successful schools in the United States frequent visits by instructional leaders to every classroom for the purpose of improving learning for all students is a day-to-day reality" (p. 2). The best instructional leaders know that time spent in classrooms is essential to understanding how to help teachers improve their teaching methods.

Getting into classrooms involves two major mind-sets. The first mind-set is that you want to be in classrooms. Believe it or not, some instructional leaders shy away from being in classrooms. They avoid the classrooms and prefer to lead from afar. That is like a hospital doctor not wanting to go into patient areas. No single instructional leadership strategy exists that can surpass time spent observing in the classroom. We usually think of classrooms as where students learn. But classrooms are also where instructional leaders learn. They learn from the teachers and the students.

Try this sometime. Pick a condition of learning that you would like to observe in action. For example, learners given time to practice and apply developing skills and strategies. Go in a number of classrooms during the week looking specifically for signs of that condition. You will be surprised what you learn or, in some cases, do not observe. This level of observation will sometimes expose gaps in teaching. For instance, you may discover that teachers, although contrary to espoused beliefs, do most of the thinking during lessons and rarely provide opportunities for students to extend and refine their thinking.

The second mind-set is that you can schedule yourself into the classroom. In other words, take charge of how you plan to spend your time. Later in this chapter, you will learn more about scheduling your most important responsibilities. For now, just the idea of getting into classrooms more often should be on your mind. To accomplish this important goal, you need to schedule classroom visitations/observations before anything else. Although getting into classrooms more frequently is certainly a challenge, the tricky part is making sure you are not disturbed once get there. Smart instructional leaders find ways to protect their time in classrooms. One way that has worked well for years is described below.

Call Backs Can Protect Your Time in Classrooms

It is bad enough that many instructional leaders regret not being able to spend more time in classrooms. The last thing you want is to be disturbed when you are finally in a classroom. With this is mind, call backs are for principals, assistant principals, and other instructional leaders who have clerical assistance. It will not let you down as a way to guard time in classrooms. What follows below is a description of the call-back process.

At the end of each workweek, schedule your classroom visitations/observations for the upcoming week. Schedule classroom visitations/observations the way you schedule meetings and other appointments. The difference is that you schedule yourself in the classroom FIRST. Make sure your secretary (clerical assistant) has your schedule for the week (computer-based or hard copy). Instruct your secretary that when you are in a classroom you are not to be disturbed for any reason unless there is an emergency OR if certain people call. That means you will need to define an emergency and identify the people who can interrupt.

Here is an example:

1. Emergencies
   a. Students or adults threatened
   b. Fire
   c. Bomb threat

2. Examples of nonemergencies
   a. Student sent to the office for a discipline matter (they will have to see someone else or wait until I return)
   b. Student sprains ankle on the playground (call nurse)

  c. Walk-in parent wanting to speak with me (make an appointment for them to see me)

 3. Who can interrupt me*

  a. My parents

  b. My spouse

---

*Notice that not even the superintendent is on the interrupt list.

When the secretary receives a call from someone not on the interrupt list (e.g., a parent) she tells that person that, "Mr. _____ is in a classroom observing instruction until (states the time). He will make call backs at such-and-such a time. Your name will be put on a call-back list, and Mr. _____ will make those calls when he returns to the office." The secretary puts the call-back list on the leader's desk, and when he returns to the office, he calls the people in the order received. When there is a true emergency in the school, the secretary alerts the leader using a signal known only to the leader.

"Being able to directly experience/see how students respond to different approaches to teaching gives a very clear picture of the impact of teaching." ~ Jay

KNOWLEDGE, NOT PACKAGED PROGRAMS

Why is it that so many education leaders believe the answer to an instructional problem can be found in a program? Whether it is a program for learning, a program for teaching, a program for reading, a program for strategic planning, a grading program, an assessment program, a writing system, or a program that differentiates, the search for just the right program is endless. Something far more important than programs exists that can improve teaching.

As an instructional leader, you need to understand the *human program*. It is the knowledge that you and the teachers have about teaching and learning that will make the difference for students, not some commercially prepared program. For instance, teachers have to know how students learn best and how to make learning more exciting and interesting for students. This will help teachers to motivate students and construct more meaningful learning opportunities. Knowledge of teaching and learning should lead instructional planning, allowing teachers to make adjustments according to student needs. Knowledge is the foundation of good lesson planning, not drill-and-skill teaching programs.

For their part, instructional leaders must have enough educational expertise to know the difference between a lesson taught at a high level versus a lesson taught at a low level. Without this competency, instructional leaders will not be able to pinpoint the need for instructional improvement. Your job as an instructional leader is to inspire and nurture knowledge building. To do this, you should put teaching on the front burner. Come out from behind the program curtain and realize that there is no *wizard of education*. An in-depth knowledge of teaching surpasses anything that can be achieved by implementing someone else's ideas. This assertion will be explored in detail in Chapter 4.

> "Education is about the students and what they need to be successful. It's not about getting through a curriculum."
> ~ Anita

LEARNING FROM MASTER TEACHERS

In the world of music, there is a process known as the *Master Class*. This is when an accomplished artist (e.g., first cello player from a philharmonic orchestra) meets with a group of cellists who are accomplished in their own right, but are not yet considered masters. They are students who want to learn more from a master. A master class is about helping musicians improve their playing, which makes the process used in a master class valuable for helping teachers to improve their teaching.

The protocol is simple. The master invites a person to play while he or she listens intently and observes her technique. The master may sometimes interrupt to make a particular point or offer suggestion. When the piece is finished (usually about 10 minutes), the master begins a feedback process that goes something like this:

- Thanks the person for playing.
- Honors the intention of the piece in very specific terms.
- Breaks the piece down by demonstrating on his or her own cello.
- Makes sure the student understands the detailed feedback (may draw a picture or demonstrate).
- Invites the student to repeat an earlier section, but this time using the master's suggestion.
- Throughout the session the master asks the person very specific questions.
- The session ends when the master once again thanks the participant and asks a new person to step forward.

The most intriguing feature of the master-class environment is how the master gives feedback. At times, the feedback borders on being blunt, but not cruel. The master chooses words very carefully but is direct and straightforward. For example, the master might say, "You cannot play that phrase so quickly and expect to capture the rhythm of the piece. You must slow down and let that melody sink in. Do not rush it. Feel it down in your toes."

The master-class environment has definite potential for educators. First, it could be used to give instructional leaders and teachers an opportunity to learn together from a master teacher in action. This is not your typical demonstration where someone in the school (e.g., instructional coach) models a lesson for teachers. Instead, it is an example of exemplary teaching usually not seen by many teachers. Two conditions must be present for this process to work: (1) the master teacher must teach the lesson to a typical class of students (i.e., mixed abilities, normal class size, and same amount of lesson time), and (2) there must be sufficient time for the master teacher and the observers to participate in a post-lesson discussion. Decisions about the nature of the lesson should be determined by the needs of the teachers. For example, a group of science teachers may wish to see an inquiry-based science lesson. Those teachers, along with an instructional leader, would be the only people observing the master lesson.

The invited master teacher should be paid and allowed to decide whether the lesson can be taped. Recorded lessons are an excellent way to build a professional library of teaching. The library gives teachers much needed access to highly effective teaching. With the changes in performance evaluations that are on the horizon, many teachers will want to see what highly effective teaching looks like.

Since it is nearly impossible to arrange for a master-class environment during regular school hours, you may need to schedule it as a half-day professional development session. A class of students would be invited to participate and receive a special thank-you for helping (e.g., lunch or special permission). A master class could also be held in conjunction with summer school.

A master-class environment could be used in a different way when working with inexperienced teachers. With this approach, an instructional leader recognized by colleagues as being a master teacher would work with a teacher one-on-one in his classroom. Emerging teachers may have never seen exemplary teaching. The process provides an excellent foundation for a rich discussion about good teaching and the possible difference with current practice.

The teacher would teach a planned lesson with the master teacher as the only observer. No one else would see this lesson, and the lesson would not be a part of a formal or informal observation. As soon as possible after the lesson, the master teacher and the classroom teacher would meet to discuss the lesson. The protocol for that conversation is modeled after the process used with a master class in music. Table 2.1 below includes the major components of this protocol with an example for each component.

Table 2.1

Protocol Components	Examples
Acknowledge what the teacher did, sometimes even offering praise.	You were modeling your process as a content-area reader summarizing a paragraph from a student text.
Honor the intention of the lesson even though the results may not have been the best.	You were trying to get all of the students to summarize their social studies reading.
Give clear constructive feedback that is free from jargon and heavy on specifics.	Instead of saying that the students were engaged, try saying, "The students were actively taking notes when you were demonstrating how you summarize."

(Continued)

Table 2.1 (Continued)

Protocol Components	Examples
Emphasize the *why* behind the *how* of teaching, but keep it simple.	Students have to see models of a good summary so they can see those same qualities in their own summary writing.
Help bring the teacher to the next level, not the top of the ladder, just up a rung or two.	Suggest going back to the lesson where the teacher asked the students to draw an inference from a paragraph in the text. What other options did you have at this point in your teaching?

The important thing here is that the teacher is receiving very specific feedback about her teaching from someone who really knows how to teach. Although this highly individualized approach to improving teaching is difficult to provide on a large scale, it is often exactly what is needed to help a promising, but struggling, teacher reach a higher level of competency. A teacher who is fortunate enough to work with a master teacher will never be the same teacher. She will look at her lesson planning, methods, delivery of instruction, and student assessments differently. The value is long-lasting for both her students and her teaching.

"Encourage teachers to visit classrooms of successful teachers and give them time to talk about what they saw and to learn together." ~ Anita

LEARNING FROM STUDENTS

Students teach educators. Educators need to observe, listen, work alongside students, and look at their work. Here is a simple plan to help you learn from students. It is based on the observational techniques pioneered by Guba and Lincoln (1981) and incorporates multiple perspectives of observation used by researchers.

1. *Detached Observer*—neutral role

   Listen to and observe a learning event, but do not actively participate. For example, sit in the library-media center and watch fifth graders access and process information or walk into a teacher's classroom and observe students working on a project.

2. *Participant Observer*—active role

    a. Listen and observe while actually participating or interacting in the learning event. For example, write with students during a social studies lesson or do the experiment in the science lab.

    b. Interview students to learn more about how they are thinking—for example, their thinking about democracy, regrouping with subtraction, or immigration laws.

3. *Collector of Artifacts*—neutral role

    Collect evidence of learning progress through records, audio and video tapes, multimedia, tests, projects, and student work samples. For example, collect and review records of oral reading behaviors or writing samples.

To see the value of this process, start by answering the following question: What can I learn from observing students that could help to improve teaching? Write your responses in the spaces provided below:

_____

_____

_____

_____

Next, check any of the responses listed below that echo yours:

__ Questions or concerns students have about how they are learning

__ What teaching methods are really working for students

__ What opportunities do students need in order to learn better

__ Where teaching methods are not effective for students

__ Ideas students have for improving teaching

__ Challenges students are facing as learners

__ Gaps in the learning process

__ Evidence of intended learning

__ Evidence from student work that instructional change is needed

__ Evidence that the school's vision statement is a reality (internal accountability)

__ Evidence that students understand what they are learning

__ Evidence that students can apply what they are learning

Using the observational techniques suggested by Guba and Lincoln (1981), you will learn more about how students are actually learning in the classroom. This in-depth understanding of how students are learning is essential to improving teaching. By concentrating on how students are learning, and not so much on how the teacher is teaching, you can observe the day-by-day reality of instruction through the eyes of the students who are on the receiving end of it.

Multiple perspectives of observation provide a rare opportunity for an instructional leader to look at teaching from the inside out. That is to say, to use what is known about how students are learning as the basis for improving the teaching. This perspective is the reverse of what is normally done to improve teaching but is closely tied to providing better learning opportunities for students, a subject that will be addressed in detail in Chapter 3.

You do not need to wait for test data or 5-week benchmarks to inform your instructional leadership practice. Keep this in mind: your instructional leadership first, and foremost, needs to be influenced by what you learn from students. Yes, test scores are a part of that understanding, but tests do not measure everything. As Diane Ravitch says, "Not everything that matters can be quantified" (2010, p. 226). Sharpen your skills of observation, and use what you discover over time in the classroom to shape the direction needed for improving teaching. As was previously mentioned, in the eyes of teachers, the credibility of an instructional leader is often based on what she knows about how students learn. The place to learn more is in the classroom.

> "The focus should be on what the students are doing and on the evidence that intended learning is taking place. Students teach us what they need if we would just pay closer attention. Learners are our ultimate teachers." ~ Ardis

NOT ENOUGH TIME?

Two areas where many instructional leaders express dissatisfaction about their work are time management (or the lack of it) and overcoming resistance to change. Since overcoming resistance to change will be addressed later on in the book, the time is right to tackle time management. This section is the most hands-on, how-to part of the entire book. It requires a level of committed action and follow-through. It will not be easy, but the results may please you. No slick strategies here—just straightforward thinking and doing.

Inquiry into time management starts with a simple question: Can time be managed? Think carefully before you answer this question because how you answer it will determine the direction you will need to take. A simple "yes" or "no" written in the margin will suffice. If you answered "no," continue to read on. If you answered "yes," skip ahead to the subheading labeled "I Answered Yes."

When you answered "no," you are saying that you do not believe that time can be managed. Perhaps a better question is, "What do we mean by time management?" Let us start there. What do you mean by time management? How you define time management, is of course, influenced by how you actually use your time. It is your philosophy in action, so to speak. So look at your philosophy in action. Here are a few simple questions that may help you do that. Check "agree" or "disagree" after each statement.

1. To be effective, I have to have a flexible time schedule. I have to be able to go with the flow. __agree / __disagree

2. Like everyone else, I schedule important things, but I do not get shook up if I have to cancel or change my schedule if something more important comes up. __agree __disagree

3. I usually have no trouble delegating certain responsibilities to make time for more important things. __agree / __disagree

4. I usually have sufficient time during the day to concentrate on important matters and get my work done. __agree / __disagree

5. At the end of the day, I usually feel good about the way I used my time for instructional matters like getting into classrooms or meeting with teaching teams. __agree / __disagree

Based on your responses and what you know about yourself, how do you define time management? Do you see it as a flexible system that reacts to the needs of the day, or do you see it as a more rigid system that allows you to plan for what is most important? Maybe your definition of time management is somewhere in between flexible and rigid. However you define time management, it will not change how you feel about the results. The balance you seek between how you use time and the satisfaction it brings you is key to your success as an instructional leader. If you are truly satisfied with how you use time, congratulations, but many instructional leaders are not. If, however, you are not content with how you use time, perhaps the three suggestions presented near the end of this section will be of interest to you.

I Answered Yes

By answering "yes," you are saying that you do believe that time can be managed. The reason you answered "yes" is probably because you have done just that—tried to manage your time. That does not mean you are satisfied, it just means that you have attempted to manage your time better. The five questions below may help you to better understand your time management needs.

1. Are you pleased with the amount of time that you spend on instructional matters? __yes / __no

2. Do you usually feel relaxed, not rushed or starved for time? __ yes / __no

3. Are you pleased with the amount of time you spend in classrooms? __ yes / __no

4. Are you usually able to concentrate on important matters? __ yes / __no

5. Do you usually control your daily schedule? __yes / __no

So how did you do? If you had five yes's (and you were brutally honest) it looks like you are handling your time just fine. Congratulations! If you had a few no's, however, keep reading. Most instructional leaders struggle with the use of their time. So, you are in good company. But, some instructional leaders are better time managers than others. Think of the best manager of time that you work with. Jot his or her name down in the margin. Then, make an appointment to talk with this person. But, before the appointment, try to predict what he or she will say when you ask this question: What are your secrets for effective time management? What you learn from talking with this person may help you address your own time-management needs. If not, what follows are two proven suggestions for maximizing time spent on improving instruction.

Suggestion #1: Take Charge of Your Schedule

Think of your schedule as the number-one way to prevent wasted time. Here is the golden rule: First, I schedule the most important things I need to be doing, and then I schedule what everyone else wants me to do. To be efficient and effective, you must build and control your own schedule. Guard it and let the people you work with know how important it is to your success as an instructional leader. If you delegate scheduling to someone else, she must know your ground rules. For example, all matters related to instruction, starting with classroom visitations/observations, have priority. All the talk about an open door policy and being accessible will interfere with you doing the things you are paid to do—namely, improve the learning opportunities for students.

For some reason, many instructional leaders find it difficult to take charge of their schedule. Even when they have it all arranged for a classroom visit, they are quick to adjust their time to meet the needs of others and then complain about not being in classrooms enough. You cannot manage your time effectively if you will not stick to your schedule. That means having to make quick decisions about the problems that come your way, sometimes referred to as handling the "monkeys."

Suggestion #2: Keep the Monkeys Off Your Back (adapted from Oncken & Wass, 1999)

Picture this. An instructional leader is walking down the hallway and a teacher stops her to talk about a problem she is having sharing textbooks in the department. You are in a hurry, so you say, "I cannot handle this right now, but I will get back to you." The "monkey" is the problem under discussion. In this example, the problem is sharing textbooks in the department. The teacher had the monkey (i.e., problem), but when you said, "I will get back to you," the monkey leaped from the teacher's back to yours.

In this instance, the instructional leader became responsible for the care and feeding of the problem (i.e., the monkey), instead of the rightful owner, the teacher. Multiply this several times a day, and you can see where some of your precious time goes, namely, doing other people's work. What mistake did the instructional leader make? She made the mistake of assuming that a problem brought to her by a teacher was a joint problem. Now the teacher can relax a bit and just wait until the instructional leader finds time to give the monkey back to her.

What could this instructional leader have done to keep the monkey off her back? She needed to say to the teacher in the hallway, "What do you think? Why don't you send me a brief note about the textbook problem with your suggestion for solving it?" The message to the teacher is: do not bring me problems; bring me solutions. Of course, there will be times when this will not be enough, but it is a start.

The authors offer several rules for keeping your monkey population to a minimum. Here are two of the best:

1. "Either feed monkeys or shoot them. A monkey who is allowed to starve to death will take up even more of your time while you dissect him to determine the cause of death or attempt to resuscitate him." A quick resolution means deciding right away who will solve the problem. Procrastination means that you view the situation as a joint problem and you will spend even more time monkeying around with it.

2. "Never feed monkeys by email. This is just another way of letting the monkey successfully leap onto your back. Instead, do it face-to-face." An email exchange will do nothing but prolong the time it takes to resolve the problem and make the problem giver feel like you are going to help solve it. Go see the person and make it clear who is responsible for handling the problem.

TRY IT IN THE CLASSROOM

New Zealand education leaders have a saying they use when they are asking teachers to implement new practices in the classroom, "Give it a go yourself!" What they mean, of course, is that the leader needs to be trying new practices in the classroom right along with the teachers. This is especially true when the practice being implemented is not in the strike zone of most teachers. Below is a case illustration that demonstrates why there is truth in the old saying: "Easier said than done."

 ## #1: Why Can't Students Grasp Basic Concepts?

Teachers in an urban district were being asked to modify their lessons in accordance with prominent research on how students learn best. In particular, middle and secondary teachers were being asked to begin each unit of study by engaging prior understandings. So, for example, if a teacher was introducing a social studies unit on conflict in the Middle East, they were expected to address students' preconceptions (and misconceptions) about the Middle East on day one. Future lessons would be shaped by what the teachers learned from this assessment of understanding.

Studies conducted by the National Research Council (2005) have shown that students come to the classroom with preconceptions about how the world works. New understandings are constructed from a foundation of existing understandings and experience. Prior learning is a powerful support for further learning. Misconceptions, however, can be just as powerful a barrier to new learning. Exposing and building on the prior knowledge of students requires more in-depth planning on the part of the teacher.

In this case, the teachers had little or no experience addressing their students' preconceptions. Despite extensive professional development and ongoing classroom-based support and guidance, the teachers continued to struggle. The instructional leadership team was baffled, and some leaders even wondered if the problem was teacher resistance. After all, the teachers had to put a lot more time and effort into their unit planning and their plans were being discussed openly. Not believing that the teachers were dragging their heels, one instructional leader suggested that perhaps engaging students' prior understandings is more difficult than anticipated. She volunteered to try it in the classroom herself.

She worked with a science teacher who was about to introduce a unit on the Planet Earth. The instructional leader would plan and teach the first-day lesson for the new unit. She would address preconceptions about two major concepts: shape of the Earth and motions of the Earth. The instructional leader planned with the science teacher but taught the lesson alone during the entire 45-minute period.

The instructional leader met with the rest of the instructional leadership team to report her findings. The science teacher attended the meeting. The instructional leader had this to say about her inquiry-based teaching experience:

1. The planning took much longer than expected. There was very little available on how to engage students' prior understandings. It took several hours to develop experiences that would address preconceptions about the shape and motions of the Earth.

2. The teaching did not go smoothly despite the planning.
   a. I was unsure of where the lesson was going and lost my sense of confidence as a teacher.
   b. The students were confused by the discussion of preconceptions and misconceptions about the Earth. Some of the students even asked what we were doing.
   c. I experienced difficulty collecting all of the data as students' prior understandings were widespread.

3. Somewhat clear about where to go next with this unit.
   a. Many students had misconceptions about the motions of the Earth, especially related to the seasons. This area will need a lot more attention than originally planned.
   b. I was not sure how to respond to the varying degrees of misconceptions about the Earth. Maybe there is a need for more small-group instruction.

Members of the instructional leadership team learned a good lesson from this experience. They realized that despite their best efforts, a lot more was needed to help the teachers implement research-based teaching. By having one of their members try it in the classroom, they were able to discover what needed to be done in order to support teachers trying to engage students' prior understandings. Clearly, this was an expectation that was easier said than done.

JOURNAL REFLECTION

Take time to write in your journal. On pages 34 and 35 are some suggestions for possible topics and subtopics to write about, including *Big Picture, Credibility, Learning,* and *In Classrooms.* Select the one that you believe will provide the greatest insights into your work now.

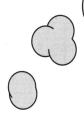

**In-Your-Head-Quiz #3
(answer on page 221)**

In August 2003, Richard Elmore submitted a report to the National Governors Association Center for Best Practices.

According to the report, which one of the four factors listed below did Elmore identify as a significant problem in struggling schools?

1. Leaders are working hard but not collaborating with teachers.

2. Teachers are working hard but not teaching based on the needs of students.

3. Teachers are working hard but not teaching for meaning and learning.

4. Teachers are working hard but not integrating the state's academic standards.

GETTING THE RIGHT THINGS DONE

 Peter Drucker spent his adult life studying leadership, especially executive leadership. In his latest book, *The Effective Executive in Action,* Drucker stated that "effectiveness can be learned" (p. 1).

Drucker discovered that effectiveness is getting the right things done. His research showed that getting the right things done consists of five complex practices:

1. Managing your time;

2. Focusing your efforts on making contributions;

3. Making your strengths productive;

4. Concentrating your efforts on those tasks that are most important to contributions; and

5. Making effective decisions.

From his in-depth research and vast experience, Drucker concluded that "these practices are simple, deceptively so. But these practices are exceedingly hard to do well" (2006, p. 1).

Big Picture

When you think about doing the right things as an instructional leader, has this part of the book validated any aspects of your work?

- How so?

Credibility

Being credible in the eyes of the teachers and staff is essential for an instructional leader. If the teachers believe you know what you are talking about and you follow through on what you say, your chances of success are good. Take a few minutes to think about your credibility.

- How do you think the teachers and staff perceive you as an instructional leader?

- Why?
- Is there anything you need to do to increase your standing with teachers and staff?

Learning

Have you been learning from students or master teachers?

- What have you learned?
- How has this learning made you a better instructional leader?

In Classrooms

- Do you get into classrooms every day?
- If not, why is that?
- More than anything else, what is the one thing you need to do in order to spend more time in classrooms?

Added Thought

You cannot beat yourself up about whether or not you are always doing the right things. The context of your work is not motionless and certainly not predictable. The unexpected happens, and rarely is there a day that some student or staff problem does not interfere with what you had planned to do. But, it does not stop there. How you reconcile what you do as an instructional leader can only come from your own sense of satisfaction. As mentioned previously (and will continue to be reinforced in the chapters ahead), your level of satisfaction will determine the degree of response to the realities of your job.

For instance, if you find you are shortchanging time in the classroom, then you will have to decide what action, if any, you plan to take to reduce that frustration. It is not a matter of knowing what to do; rather, it is a matter of getting yourself to do it. There are no simple solutions to how you approach your work as an instructional leader. But, obviously there is a good reason for wanting to do the right things. That reason is to help teachers learn more about teaching so they can provide the best learning opportunities possible for students. In the spirit of Peter Drucker, this is what an instructional leader is paid to do.

TRY THIS: MATTER OVER TIME

The essence of Chapter 2 is whether you are doing the right things. Getting the right things done will increase your effectiveness as an instructional leader.

But, what if you are still having trouble spending time on the leadership responsibilities that you know are crucial to improving teaching and learning?

 Try THIS:

- Make a list of the five most important things you should be doing every day to be considered a "highly effective" instructional leader by your peers.
- Put these five things that are crucial to your success on an index card. Keep the card with you at all times.
- With your card as your motivation, pick a day and totally change your normal routine. If you never observe a lesson during the first period, do that. Make sure your schedule is completely different.
- Be prepared to fight the impulse to revert to your old routine. It will be a strong impulse, and you will not feel comfortable trying to change.
- At the end of the day, think about what you did. If you did not stick to your new schedule, try it again on another day.
- What have you learned that may help you to do the right things?

 ## LEADERSHIP TEAM ACTIVITY

Learning From Students

Purpose

Start with the end in mind.

- Administrators and teacher leaders will gain a better understanding of their roles as instructional leaders when they think about their work through the eyes of their students.
- Visualize the action needed to transfer seminar learning and understanding to current instructional leadership practice.

Perspective

- Educators talk all the time about being there for the students, but how often do teachers and administrators really listen to what the students have to say about the teaching-learning process?

Challenge

- To be truly effective, an instructional leader must possess an accurate understanding of the students—not just their academic knowledge and skills—but how students really feel about the process we call "school."

Plan

The basic steps for facilitating this single-focus seminar:

1. Prior to the seminar:
   a. Arrange for a group of 10, mixed-ability students (age appropriate) to participate in a roundtable discussion about school.
   b. Select a person unknown to the students to moderate the discussion.
   c. Have the leadership team develop 6 to 10 questions to guide the discussion. The questions should have value for an instructional leader.
   d. Videotape the roundtable discussion in such a way that the identity of the students cannot be known.
2. Provide time for a 60-minute seminar session with the leadership team.
   a. Watch the video together, stopping for reactions and clarification (invite the moderator to attend to add additional insight into the process).

Personal and Team Connections

- Participants will be asked to connect their unique leadership challenges to the content of the seminar.
- The team will ask two essential questions: (1) What have we been learning? (2) How can we use this learning to strengthen our work as instructional leaders?

BRIDGE TO CHAPTER 3

Think of doing the right things as a framework for increasing effectiveness as an instructional leader. These *habits of practice* become automatic and are centered on improving teaching. Doing the right things is another step toward closing the teaching gap. Remember that you need to be in charge of what you do, how you use your time, and the priorities you set for improving teaching. Learn from the people you serve—the students and teachers. Because students and teachers spend most of their days in classrooms, you need to be in there with them as much as possible. When you help teachers learn from their experience and problems of practice, you are building capacity for a base of knowledge that can increase student learning.

Chapter 3 offers an important distinction between teaching methods and learning opportunities for students. Instructional leaders must be able to help teachers understand that while there are many effective teaching methods, students' learning opportunities might need to change. The goal is making progress toward closing the teaching gap. Better learning opportunities for students are not created in a vacuum. They are created in the culture of teaching that is present in every school. The culture of teaching is often the dependent variable when it comes to improving teaching and learning.

In this chapter, there will be a great deal of emphasis put on the importance of matching practice with a shared vision of learning and teaching. Beliefs about learning should ground the selection of teaching methods throughout a school. Clear articulation of a theory of effective instruction is an essential aspect of any school. Although teachers may not all use the same teaching methods, the methods they do use should be based on how students learn best.

Because the culture of teaching is often like a puzzle with missing pieces, you will be given access to a new tool for analyzing your school's culture of teaching. This instrument will help you to better understand some of the forces at work that make it difficult to improve teaching. Having a deeper understanding of the culture of teaching is an advantage for instructional leaders helping teachers to create better learning opportunities for students.

CHAPTER THREE

Creating Better Learning Opportunities for Students

"Teaching quality needs to be defined not by what teachers do but by the learning opportunities they create for students. Improving teaching is the single most effective step we can take to improve student learning."

—James Stigler (October 6, 2009)

TEACHING METHODS AND LEARNING OPPORTUNITIES

James Stigler provides the perspective for Chapter 3 by shifting the focus from the methods and techniques employed by teachers to the nature of the learning opportunities made available to students. Instead of concentrating on what the teacher is doing, Stigler urges educators to pay more attention to how the students are learning. In other words, there are many effective teaching methods, but the teacher must be able to select the methods that will provide the best opportunity for students to learn.

The relevance of this perspective is easier to grasp when it is presented in a realistic context. For example, at some point in time, all students learn about weather in school. Therefore, the study of weather provides a useful lens for looking at the difference between teaching methods and learning opportunities for students. Many ways exist to teach students about weather.

In one seventh-grade classroom, the teacher had his students read the latest books about weather and complete the various weather activities found online at http://www.fi.edu/weather/activity.html. In another seventh-grade classroom, the teacher had her students make weather instruments and use them to set up a weather station in the classroom and on the school grounds. The students developed daily weather reports that were broadcast every morning over the school's public address system. It is not a question of which method is better. The question is what learning opportunity is better for students? The focus changes from standards of outcomes to standards of opportunity.

Students in both classrooms were given opportunities to learn about weather but in different ways. The students in the first classroom (textbooks and Internet) were learning what someone else had discovered and developed about weather. This is a more traditional approach to learning. The students in the second classroom (instruments and weather station) were learning about weather through a process of discovery and applying new learning in ways that were relevant in their lives (e.g., weather forecasting). This approach to learning is more about discovery and understanding.

What Is Meant by Better Learning Opportunities?

Creating better learning opportunities for students is not synonymous with the teaching methods chosen by a teacher. The quality of an educational opportunity depends on a teacher's understanding of how students learn best and the teacher's ability to convert that understanding into the appropriate conditions for learning. Although methods may vary from one teacher to another, there is one constant—the quality of the learning opportunities available to all students.

Creating better learning opportunities for students depends on the belief systems about learning and the skills of leaders (teachers and administrators) to implement desired practice within the existing culture of teaching and the realities of the status quo. When instructional leaders are helping teachers create better learning opportunities for students, they are closing the teaching gap. Creating better learning opportunities for students does not mean getting better at teaching narrowly focused subject matter that prepares students for standardized tests but does little to inspire or motivate students to want to learn. Better learning opportunities are creative and exciting and often prompt students to want to learn more. They bring out the joy of learning and the pride in teaching. Creating better learning opportunities for students is the heart and soul of a new conception of teaching.

The case illustration that follows underscores the difficulties faced by an instructional leader who is expecting teachers to create better learning opportunities for students. As you go through the case, keep in mind that Richard Elmore, Peterson, and McCarthey (1996), after an in-depth study of restructuring schools, concluded that enthusiasm for new visions does not automatically lead people to see the implications for teaching. They found that it is very difficult for educators to attain the deep, systematic knowledge of practice needed to make the vision a reality.

#2: A Rose by Any Other Name

Juan Salvatore is the principal of a K–5 elementary school in the Hispanic/Latino section of an urban community. Juan has been at the school throughout his career as a teacher, teacher leader, assistant principal, and, now, principal. Juan knows every family in the school and they know him. Many of the teachers are Hispanic/Latino and could best be described as traditional in their approach to teaching. They are solid teachers who prefer the familiarity and security of a structured curriculum, scripted textbooks, and fun activities for students to do. They have high expectations for student behavior and effort.

The results of the reading and mathematics standardized tests taken by the children in Grades 3–5 over the past 3 years indicate the following patterns:

- Listening and speaking have improved considerably
- Decoding skills and vocabulary are fine; difficulty comprehending nonfiction expository pieces

- Struggling with grammar and spelling
- Narrative writing is good; nonfiction writing is not so good
- Know their number facts and computational skills; difficulty with problem-solving

Juan was concerned about this pattern because it revealed a need for a more precise approach to teaching and learning. He called a faculty meeting the second week of September to express his concerns and to seek input from the teachers. He insisted that this was a challenge for all teachers, not just Grades 3–5.

Working in table groups, the teachers were asked to analyze the situation from their point of view in the classroom. Were they seeing the same learning discrepancies? Each table group summarized their main points on chart paper, which they shared with the group. The similarities between the groups were convincing. The crux of the problem was nonfiction reading and writing. It showed up in all core academic subjects.

After the meeting, the teachers at each grade level put together a plan for improving nonfiction reading and writing. Plans included more time spent on nonfiction, integrating strategy instruction into the core academic subjects, using a wider variety of nonfiction materials (e.g., books, booklets, brochures, and content-based magazines), and more teacher demonstrations followed by guided practice. Everyone seemed to be charged!

By the middle of October, Juan began making his instructional rounds to see how the teachers were getting on with some of their ideas for improving nonfiction reading and writing. In room after room, Juan saw teaching pretty much unchanged. Students were still being drilled on basic math facts, using word walls (although expanded to include more nonfiction words), reading in round-robin fashion, and solving problems using the teacher's step-by-step approach, and there was little evidence that teachers were demonstrating strategies in the content areas. What had happened to the enthusiasm for creating better learning opportunities for students?

The work of creating better learning opportunities for students is only half done when the teachers and the instructional leader understand the needs of the students. In this case, the principal and the teachers understood that the students needed more help with nonfiction reading and writing. The problem was that the teachers did not know how to integrate strategy instruction into their core academic lessons. Therefore, they fell back to their old ways of teaching.

HOW DO STUDENTS LEARN BEST?

> *"A mission-critical challenge, then, is for schools to construct a way for all staff members to come to deeply understand and make learning principles their own."*
>
> —Wiggins and McTighe, 2007 (p. 121)

Below is a simple but proven protocol for putting you in touch with how you learn best. After you have completed this exercise, do not be surprised if your perspective on how students learn best is somewhat altered.

- Think of something you recently learned (personal or professional). It could be learning a second language, developing a web page, keeping score at a baseball game, making a new pattern for a dress, baking bread from scratch, or writing an editorial for the newspaper.
- I learned to_____
- Write down everything you can think of that helped you to learn how to do it.

_____

_____

_____

_____

- Take a moment to reflect on conditions that help you as a learner. Are they the same conditions that help students to learn in the classroom?

Student Learning

"I never teach my pupils; I only attempt to provide the conditions in which they can learn."

—Albert Einstein

How do students learn? That is the basic question we need to ask ourselves as educators. A major premise put forth in this book is that learning opportunities for students should be driven by how students learn best. Is that possible?

Look around your school or district. Is the teaching driven by how students learn best? Maybe it depends on how you and the teachers think students learn best.

The dialogue below may shed some light on this quandary. It comes from a discussion involving three fifth-grade teachers and their principal. It was a casual table conversation prompted by an exercise presented during a professional seminar.

PRINCIPAL: So, how do we think students learn best?

TEACHER A: They have to see a purpose in what they are doing. Students learn best when the learning is real. Relevancy is so important. They have to experience the learning in order to fully understand and apply it.

TEACHER B: That may be true for some, but most students need to know exactly what they will be learning and then have it taught directly. I hate to say this, but students are sort of like empty vessels and we have to fill them with knowledge. Without knowledge, they cannot apply what have learned.

PRINCIPAL: I can only think about how I learn. It helps me when someone shows me what to do and then gives me time and support to try it myself. It is this gradual release of responsibility from teacher to student that helps kids learn best.

TEACHER C: My kids learn better when they are working together and have hands-on discovery activities.

Students need to think things through. Experience is not enough. They love to figure things out, and it gets them excited about the learning. Students learn best by answering their own questions.

PRINCIPAL: Do you think as a staff we need to be more consistent in our beliefs about how students learn best?

Consistency or Autonomy?

The principal's last question was right on, but complex. Do teachers and instructional leaders need to have a shared belief system about how students learn best? Educators belong to a profession that has long thrived on autonomy. Teachers and instructional leaders often cringe at being told what to do and how to do it. But something has been missing from this debate—the impact on students.

As students go through school, they move from teacher to teacher. As students move up in the grades, it is not unusual for them to have five or six different teachers in a day. Some of those teachers will have similar beliefs about how students learn, but some will not. Just ask the students. As early as fourth grade, students can begin telling you how their teachers believe students learn best.

To be absolutely clear about this, a shared understanding of how students learn best is not about getting all the teachers to use the same teaching methods. There are many effective ways to teach. For example, if teachers believe that inquiry-based learning is best for students, it does not mean that it has to be done in laboratory or small-group work. This approach to learning can also be done in lectures that provoke students to think and question. Collaborative meaning-making can take place through discussion.

Creating better learning opportunities for students is not so much about the teaching method as it is about how the teachers view learning. The important thing to understand here is that even when methods vary from teacher to teacher, students benefit when the learning principles upon which those teaching methods are envisioned, developed, and delivered remain a constant in every classroom. If teachers believe students benefit from seeing a demonstration or being given an example, then this condition of learning is incorporated into their teaching no matter which methods they use. Students in teacher-centered and student-centered classrooms have the opportunity to learn from demonstrations and examples. This is consistency in beliefs about learning.

Is the reverse also true? Can variations in beliefs about how students learn best be a negative factor? For some students that seems possible. Say, for example, some students learn better when they are allowed to work with classmates. But, how do these students learn in classrooms where they are not allowed to work together? Will their learning suffer? Parents deal with this actuality all the time and often tell their kids: "Look, you can't always learn the way you want to in every class. You have to adjust to each learning situation. That is just the way it is in school, so get used to it."

Imagine if a hospital operated that way. The patient in room 5001C would just have to adjust to the fact that the nurse working in that room does not believe medications should be regulated over time. That nurse would leave it up to the patient to decide when to take his or her medication.

Consistency in beliefs about learning has the best chance of guiding teaching that reflects those beliefs. Minus this consistency in beliefs, the teaching practice may be all over the map. This is not the direction needed to begin closing the gap in teaching.

"Administrators and teachers must have similar ideas on how to deliver instruction based on how students learn."
~ Jay

METHODS VERSUS BELIEFS

It is important here to differentiate between methods and beliefs. Beliefs support the methods and techniques that teachers use. Beliefs are based on principles of learning developed from years of experience and research. For example, lecturing is a teaching method. Teachers lecture because they believe students need to build background in order to better understanding difficult concepts and make connections to new learning.

Most teachers use a variety of methods in their teaching. These methods, however, are greatly determined by their beliefs about learning. A teacher who rarely lectures to students may tell you that she believes that learning should be active. Her beliefs about learning are dictating her methods. The selection of teaching methods for some teachers is a matter of doing what they have experienced themselves as learners in school. The researchers Stigler and Hiebert (1999) make a strong case about the influence of the culture of teaching on the methods used by teachers. If a science teacher learned science from lectures, labs, notes, and tests, it is not surprising that he will teach that way. The opposite is also true; a science teacher who learned science by discovery and inquiry-based instruction is more apt to use these methods in his teaching.

Ironically, teachers whose students are scoring very high on standardized tests (e.g., elementary language arts teachers and Advanced Placement teachers) are sometimes reluctant to change methods, even when those methods are not in line with how they think students learn best. High-stakes testing puts pressure on teachers and can drive a wedge between methods and beliefs. The distance between methods used and held beliefs about student learning is a measure of the teaching gap. Using an analogy to Vygotsky's "zone of proximal development" (1978), the gap between beliefs about learning and actual teaching practice is where an instructional leader must focus her efforts.

Developing Beliefs About How Students Learn Best

Here is a way to reach staff agreement about how students learn best. You can use this collaborative decision process with a grade level, department, or entire school faculty. Teachers will need to work in small groups. The initial goal is to come up with three beliefs.

As a starter, each table group is given the same list of beliefs about how students learn best. This list provides space for teachers to add other beliefs about learning.

Our Beliefs About Learning

- Learner perceptions must be addressed directly. Understand what students are thinking, especially when beginning a new topic or unit.

- Learners must be given the opportunity to connect current knowledge with new learning. Build on what students know and can do.
- Factual information must be organized around key concepts and not learned in isolation. This promotes understanding.
- Young learners need to be immersed in all kinds of texts, fiction and nonfiction.
- Learners need to receive many demonstrations and examples. Modeling supports understanding and application.
- Learners need time and opportunity to practice, use, and apply what they have learned. Mistakes and approximations are a part of learning.
- Learners must receive feedback from more knowledgeable others. It must be timely and specific.
- Learners need to be working for a purpose and not ritual compliance such as copying notes. True engagement means students are involved in their work and try hard.
- To become self-directed learners, students must learn to monitor and adjust their approaches to learning.
- Other (e.g., learners need to take notes and listen during lectures).

_____

_____

Decision Process

1. Ask the teachers to discuss each belief and to *select only three beliefs* that they feel should *guide learning in every classroom* regardless of the teaching methods employed in that classroom.

2. Post the three beliefs from each group.

3. As a group, decide which three beliefs will guide learning in every classroom.

4. Decide together how these beliefs will be monitored to ensure that they have been translated into daily practice. This discussion will prove to be interesting.

5. After the three beliefs have been selected, all teachers involved should be given a poster for their classroom titled "How Students Learn Best." It should also be posted in the offices of the instructional leaders.

Bringing Three Beliefs Closer to Practice

Teachers may wish to subject all of the beliefs to this level of scrutiny. Help them to understand that it is better to take small steps and concentrate on just the three. The important thing to understand here is that the beliefs are shared and that there is a genuine commitment to bringing these beliefs closer to practice. This is the committed action needed to help close the teaching gap.

The systematic monitoring of the three beliefs can be done in a number of ways.

1. Teacher self-assessments

2. Lesson planning

3 Discussions at staff meetings (e.g., how beliefs are used to guide teaching)

4. Informal classroom visits

5. Observations

When questioned, most teachers will tell you that students learn things best by doing. One can only think about how much more the driver of a car learns about a particular travel route as compared with a passenger. This insight into learning makes sense and is backed up by years of educational research. So what is the problem? Classroom after classroom is dominated by inactive student *passengers* with an active teacher *driver* doing most of the thinking. We know, but we do not do.

One thing seems certain: the best teaching is underwritten by how students learn best. We kid ourselves when we think otherwise. The best opportunities for student learning do not come from teaching methods; they come from the beliefs the teachers have about how students learn best. As mentioned earlier, a lecture can be just as effective as a discovery activity, but only if the teachers believe that students have to be challenged to think and to question. Instructional leaders have a responsibility to students and parents to help teachers use important beliefs about learning to guide their lesson planning.

"I needed to understand the underlying values and beliefs that teachers had about teaching and learning; to know whether those values and beliefs were evident in the teaching I was seeing when I visited classrooms; and to know whether or not the teaching was effective." ~ Bill

THE CULTURE OF TEACHING

"Culture does not change because we desire to change it. Culture changes when the organization is transformed; the culture reflects the realities of people working together every day."

—Frances Hesselbein, 1999 (p. 6)

There is a culture of teaching in every school. It is both above ground and below ground with some obvious and some not so obvious feelings, beliefs, and attitudes that affect teaching and learning. These factors have a great deal to do with how things get accomplished in a school. The culture of teaching is the context for the work of an instructional leader attempting to close the teaching gap. Sometimes the culture of teaching in a school can be read like a book. For instance, teachers will cooperate more fully with leaders they respect and trust. Conversely, teachers will oppose the infusion of new programs when they have not been included in the decision-making process. There are times, however, when trying to figure out the culture of teaching is harder than trying to open a new jar of pickles. Instructional leaders who ignore or do not pay attention to their school's culture of teaching are in for some surprises.

The Culture of Teaching Found in Most Schools

Think of it this way: The culture of teaching in a school is the *incubator* for creating better learning opportunities for students. It is complex, dynamic, and usually does not change much. In the simplest of terms, the culture of teaching is the way most of the people think and act. To be successful, you must not only understand the habits of teaching in your school, you must be able to influence them.

Some cultures of teaching could be described as open systems. Staff do their own thing, and everyone's ideas are tolerated if not respected. Change goes almost unnoticed. Teaching looks a little different in every classroom. Conversely, some cultures of teaching are collaborative. Staff decide what to do together. Teamwork is the air they breathe. Individuality and risk taking are rare. Change is debated forever. Teaching looks much the same in each classroom.

The culture of teaching found in most schools, however, is a mix of all of the above and then some. The teachers in this type of mixed culture tend to be conservative and often appear rooted in the status quo. That is not meant to be a negative; it just describes typical group behavior. The two most frequently heard phrases are "what goes around comes around" and "been there, done that." In these cultures, groups of teachers form a strong bond. Friendships can last more than 20 years. Innovators, especially student-centered teachers, may be professionally ostracized or casually dismissed, "Oh, that is just Tom." Teaching is viewed as an individual craft, and most teachers are reluctant to make their work public. Rarely do teachers observe in each other's classrooms for the purpose of learning more about teaching. Pointed discussions about teaching are tolerated so long as the conversation does not get too close to individual practice.

Student achievement data are generally accepted if the results are presented by school, grade level, or department. Teacher-by-teacher analysis of results has not reached a level of comfort in most of these cultures of teaching. It is not uncommon for teachers to speak privately and negatively about the amount of data. Sometimes teachers in these typical cultures form alliances to advance an idea (e.g., cooperative learning) and sometimes to oppose one (e.g., differentiated learning). When the push for desired change accelerates, so does the apprehension. Folks will say, "You can feel the tension in the air." Loss of time to "work in my classroom" is the number one dissatisfier.

The teachers can be influenced or inspired by key instructional leaders to change. But it still depends on the issue. When the *right group of teachers* decide they are in favor of something, however, it sails through without a hitch. The sense of accomplishment is overwhelming and usually results in some grand celebration.

"It's important to know as much as you can about the culture of teaching. You want to be in a culture where you feel comfortable and one where you feel you will be challenged to grow professionally." ~Ardis

---

Teaching Is a Cultural Activity

Stigler and Hiebert (2009) provide convincing evidence that teaching is a complex system, and like other cultural activities, teaching is learned through active participation (both as a learner and as a teacher) over many years. They argue that in order to improve teaching, we must improve the "scripts" for teaching, that is, the mental picture of what teaching is like—the way we teach. Scripts, the authors say, "rest on a relatively small and tacit set of core beliefs about the *nature of the subject*, about *how students learn*, and about the *role that a teacher should play in the classroom*" (p. 87).

These implied beliefs, often unspoken, account for much of what a teacher does in the classroom (e.g., using visual media to focus attention rather than to record new learning, not allowing students added time to struggle with problems, essential questions, or concepts) and as such, are difficult to change merely by introducing a new program, adopting best practice, selecting an innovation, or implementing a school-improvement plan.

Instructional leaders work in a culture of teaching in much the same way that civic leaders work in a community. Civic leaders who misread their community often run the risk of failed projects and lost elections. Instructional leaders who misread their culture of teaching often run the risk of stalled improvements and the build-up of resistance to ongoing desired change. So what is the lesson for instructional leaders? The more you understand the culture in which you work, the better your chances of success. You cannot begin to close the teaching gap without this basic understanding. The culture of teaching is the starting point of instructional leadership. It is the dependent variable when it comes to selecting strategies for developing a theory of action or leading instructional improvement initiatives. The more you understand about the context of teaching, the better choices you can make as an instructional leader.

The Culture of Teaching in Your School

If you feel that your instructional leadership is like dust on a shelf, you may wish to become better informed about your school's culture of teaching. The comprehensive tool found below was developed for instructional leaders who are seeking answers to why the teaching practice in their school does not match espoused beliefs about how students learn best—the teaching gap. It includes 10 essential factors that impact the culture of teaching. The time you spend completing the matrix and analyzing the results will help you better understand the culture that surrounds the teaching in your school. To add value, ask a colleague to do it with you.

Analyzing the Culture of Teaching

Getting started:

- Think of this as a perceptual inquiry exercise. In other words, an investigation into how you perceive the culture of teaching in your school.
- After carefully considering all of the statements in each section, *use a highlighter to mark the statements in each section that you believe best describe your particular situation.*
- Each section has a place to record comments or questions that you may wish to explore further later on.
- For best results, think of *what is* rather than *what should be.*

Identifying Default Beliefs, Routines, Practices, Behaviors, and Actions
Section 1: History of School Improvement
The culture of teaching is greatly impacted by what has gone on before. People do not forget the past right away. A positive history may lead to a positive future and vice versa. It is the history of school improvement that usually accounts for comments such as: "What goes around, comes around," "We can do it if we work together," or "Been there, done that." *For each pair of statements listed below,* highlight the one that you feel best describes the **history of school improvement**.
• There is a negative history of school improvement in the school or district.
• There is a positive history of school improvement in the school or district.
• When it comes to making school improvements, there is a lack of consistency as to how it should be accomplished.
• When it comes to making school improvements, there is a level of consistency as to how it should be accomplished.
• There are many uncoordinated improvement initiatives going on at one time.
• There are very few, if any, uncoordinated improvement initiatives going on at one time.
Comments or questions:
Total positive score = 3 Our score =
Section 2: Beliefs About How Students Learn Best
The culture of teaching gradually emerges from the way teachers and administrators think about student learning. *For each pair of statements listed below,* highlight *one* statement that you feel best describes the **beliefs about how students learn best**.
• Most teachers have their own beliefs about how students learn best.
• Most teachers have similar beliefs about how students learn best.
• Most administrators have their own beliefs about how students learn best.
• Most administrators have similar beliefs about how students learn best.
Comments or questions:
Total positive score = 2 Our score =

Section 3: The Way Teachers Study Teaching
A culture in which teachers actively study teaching together may be very different from a culture where this type of collaboration is not present. *For each pair of statements listed below,* highlight ***one*** statement that you feel best describes **the way teachers study teaching**.
• There is little evidence that teachers study teaching together.
• It is very obvious that teachers study teaching together.
• Effective teaching is rarely modeled or demonstrated.
• Effective teaching is often modeled or demonstrated.
• When effective teaching is modeled or demonstrated, it is rarely discussed.
• When effective teaching is modeled or demonstrated, it is almost always discussed.
• Teachers rarely, if ever, watch multimedia lessons together.
• Teachers watch multimedia lessons together and discuss the lesson afterwards.
• Teachers rarely, if ever, watch each other teach and discuss what they are learning.
• Teachers often watch each other teach and discuss what they are learning.
Comments or questions:
Total positive score = 5 Our score =
Section 4: The Way Teachers Develop Lessons
The culture of teaching contains many of the conditions that influence how lessons are developed. *For each pair or trio of statements listed below,* highlight ***one*** statement that you feel **best describes the way teachers develop lessons.**
• Lessons are usually developed by individual teachers with occasional input from colleagues.
• Lessons are usually developed collaboratively with a great deal of input from colleagues.

(Continued)

(Continued)

• Some teachers occasionally use commercially prepared lessons. • Teachers do not use commercially prepared lessons.
• Most teachers do not write lesson plans. • Most teachers write lesson plans.
• Teachers are not required to write lesson plans. • Teachers are required to write lesson plans and must use the same lesson design/format. • Teachers are required to write lesson plans but are free to use whatever lesson design/format they wish.
Comments or questions:
Total positive score = 4 Our score =

Section 5: Two Models that Guide Teaching

Often the culture of teaching can be defined by one of two major models that drive teaching. Naturally, there are variations with both of the suggested models.

Below are two statements about two such teaching models. Highlight *one* statement that best describes the teaching model found in your school, department, team, or grade level. You may feel there is evidence of both teaching models, but **which teaching model is the one most widely practiced**?

• Teacher-directed model (direct instruction) with planning, decision-making, organization, content, methods, and assessments largely determined by the teacher(s). Aligned with standards. Student learning is less active relying on memorization and practice with the underlying belief that all students can learn if they are provided the appropriate learning conditions. The learning goal is greater mastery. The teacher acts more like an instructor than a facilitator.

• Student-centered model with planning, decision-making, organization, content, methods, and assessments largely determined by the needs and abilities of the students. Aligned with standards. Student learning is more active relying on conceptualizations, inquiry, discovery, and problem-solving with the underlying belief that students generate knowledge and meaning from their experiences. Students' questions often drive the learning. The learning goal is deeper understanding. The teacher acts more like a facilitator than an instructor.

Comments or questions:

Total positive score = 1 Our score =

Section 6: The Way Instruction Is Delivered
The culture of teaching not only has a lot to do with the way instruction is developed, but also how it is delivered. It can even be a factor in influencing teachers not to use widely acclaimed methods even when teachers think these methods are effective. *For each pair of statements listed below,* highlight the one that you feel best describes the **way instruction is delivered**.
• Mostly whole-class instruction and seat work.
• Mostly small-group instruction and seat work.
• Teachers spend most of their time teaching.
• Teachers spend most of their time assessing.
• Individualistic: The learning or achievement of one student is independent and separate from the achievements and learning of the other students in the class.
• Collaborative: The learning or achievement of all of the students is connected to the achievements and learning of the other students in the class.
• Technology is used mainly by teachers as a teaching tool (e.g., PowerPoint).
• Technology is used mainly by students as a learning tool (e.g., computer-assisted instruction).
Comments or questions:
THIS SECTION IS ASSESSED BUT NOT SCORED
Section 7: The Way Instruction Is Improved
The culture of teaching most certainly affects the way instruction is improved. It can be just as much a barrier as a source of positive support and guidance. *For each pair of statements listed below,* highlight the *one* that you feel best describes the **way instruction is improved**.
• Teachers are rarely consulted when there is a need to improve instruction.
• Teachers are always consulted when there is a need to improve instruction.

(Continued)

(Continued)

• It is rare to see teachers working collaboratively to improve instruction.
• Teachers almost always work together to improve instruction.
• Teachers work independently during or after participating in professional development.
• Teachers work together during or after participating in professional development.
• Teachers rarely work together to develop common formative and summative assessments.
• Teachers usually work together to develop common formative and summative assessments.
• Teachers often have an opportunity to work in their classroom with an instructional coach.
• Teachers almost never have an opportunity to work in their classroom with an instructional coach.
Comments or questions:
Total positive score = 5 Our score =
Section 8: How Teaching Methods Are Changed When Students Are Not Succeeding
There is no greater strain put on a culture of teaching than when students are not succeeding. The ability to take the action needed to make desired changes in teaching methods is what separates the great from the good schools. *For each set of statements listed below,* highlight the ***one*** that you feel best describes **how teaching methods are changed when students are not succeeding**.
• Even when students are not succeeding, teaching methods rarely change.
• When students are not succeeding, there is a strong likelihood that teaching methods will change.
• Teachers working alone rarely change their teaching methods.
• Teachers working alone are more apt to change their teaching methods.

- Teaching methods only change when mandated from above.
- Teaching methods change because teachers and administrators see the need for change.

- Teaching methods never change after professional development.
- Teaching methods sometimes change after professional development.
- Teaching methods always change after professional development.

- Peer pressure causes teachers to change their methods.
- Peer pressure rarely causes teachers to change their methods.

- Teaching methods seldom change because of the work of teacher-driven instructional teams.
- Teaching methods often change because of the work of teacher-driven instructional teams.

Comments or questions:

Total positive score = 6 Our score =

Section 9: How Teaching and Instructional Change Is Supported

Without ongoing support, the culture of teaching may become too weak to make or sustain desired instructional change. However, sometimes the culture of teaching can provide the conditions needed to overcome a lack of support. *For each pair of statements listed below,* highlight the *one* that you feel best describes **how teaching and instructional change is supported**.

- Teachers rarely receive face-to-face or two-way communication from their leaders, both administrators and teacher leaders.
- Teachers frequently receive face-to-face or two-way communication from their leaders, both administrators and teacher leaders.

- Teachers are rarely offered choices as to how to make desired instructional change.
- Teachers are usually offered choices as to how to make desired instructional change.

(Continued)

- Teachers rarely have sufficient time to meet together as a department, team, or grade level.
- Teachers usually have sufficient time to meet together as a department, team, or grade level.

- Teachers rarely have sufficient supplies and equipment to do their jobs adequately.
- Teachers usually have sufficient supplies and equipment to do their jobs adequately.

- Teachers are rarely provided in-class support when implementing instructional change (e.g., instructional coach or demonstration lessons).
- Teachers are usually provided in-class support when implementing instructional change (e.g., instructional coach or demonstration lessons).

- Teachers rarely work closely with instructional leaders (administrators and teacher leaders) when implementing instructional change.
- Teachers usually work closely with instructional leaders (administrators and teacher leaders) when implementing instructional change.

- Teachers rarely receive ongoing implementation and reflection support throughout the period of change.
- Teachers almost always receive ongoing implementation and reflection support throughout the period of change.

- The district rarely provides an adequate level of support (time, people, and money) for implementing instructional change.
- The district usually provides an adequate level of support (time, people, and money) for implementing instructional change.

- Even when the negotiated agreement is not being violated, the teachers bargaining unit (union) is often a negative factor where change is concerned and frequently makes it more difficult for school leaders and fellow teachers to implement desired instructional change.

• The teachers bargaining unit (union) is not a negative factor when considering instructional change and can usually be counted on to provide ongoing support and cooperation unless some aspect of the negotiated agreement is being violated.
Comments or questions:
Total positive score = 9 Our score =
Section 10: Assessments and Data
Over the years, factors related to data and assessments have greatly impacted the culture of teaching found in most schools. For better or for worse, the use of data and assessments has become embedded into the culture of teaching. *For each pair of statements listed below,* highlight *one* statement that you feel best describes **assessments and data.**
• Teachers teaching the same grade level or course of study rarely work together to develop and use common formative and summative assessments.
• Teachers teaching the same grade level or course of study usually work together to develop and use common formative and summative assessments.
• We are data driven.
• We are data informed.
Comments or questions:
Total positive score = 2 Our score =

Scoring/Assessing

- For Sections 1, 2, 3, 4, 5, and 6, each second statement highlighted equals 1 point. A total positive score would be 16 points.
- Section 6 is assessed, but *not scored.*
- For Sections 7, 8, 9, and 10, each second statement highlighted equals 1 point. A total positive score would be 22 points.
- TOTAL SCORE = _____ (37 total points)

Analysis

- For Sections 1, 2, 3, 4, and 5 (subtotal = 16)
  - A score of 14 or higher is very positive. It means that the infrastructure for your culture of teaching is in place.

- o A score of 9 to 13 is also positive, but you may want to address the areas that are lowest.
- o A score of 8 or below means that the infrastructure for your culture of teaching is lacking. Address the areas that you believe are in need of the greatest attention.
- Section 6 is especially important, as you probably are striving for a student-centered learning environment.
- For Sections 7, 8, 9, and 10 (subtotal = 22)
  - o A score of 19 or higher is very positive. It means that the actions taken in your culture of teaching support instructional improvement.
  - o A score of 11 to 18 is also positive, but you may want to address the areas that are lowest.
  - o A score of 10 or below means that your culture of teaching is probably not supporting instructional improvement. Address the areas that you believe are in need of the greatest attention.

Example of How the Analysis Works

What you learn from an analysis of the culture of teaching should be shared with other leaders in the building. Together you can use what you have discovered to pinpoint areas that may be contributing to a teaching gap. Below is an example of how this analysis worked in a middle school using Section 8: How Teaching Methods Are Changed When Students Are Not Succeeding.

The score for this section was 1 out of 6. The only positive was: "Teachers working alone are more apt to change their teaching methods." Results for this section indicated that very little change is occurring from district or school-sponsored initiatives. Teachers are not working together to modify or adjust their teaching to the needs of the students.

The instructional leader at this school decided to use these data as the basis of a meeting with some of the classroom teachers. At that meeting, the instructional leader discovered that the teachers were frustrated by years of top-down management. The teachers did not feel that they were truly involved in the decisions that affected teaching and learning. The results of this meeting had a positive effect, as both the teachers and the instructional leader agreed there was a need to give teachers a greater say in how instructional decisions were made. This led to the development of an Instructional Leadership Team made up of classroom teachers and building administrators.

CHANGING THE CULTURE OF TEACHING

 According to Evans (2001):

"Though the weight of the evidence confirms the difficulty of accomplishing true culture change, there are many who hugely underestimate the task. Since schools are by their very nature less entrepreneurial and more bureaucratic and since most are mature rather than new institutions, the gravitational pull of culture is stronger in them." (p. 50)

"Not only should we see school culture as a force acting against change, we should also remember that this opposition is sensible, even when the necessity for change may seem compelling from an external perspective. Thus we find repeated at the collective level the same conservative impulse we saw among individuals—an impulse as vital as it is profound and which reform, if it is to success, must respect." (p. 50)

"We can see that our system of schooling needs improvement in many areas. I have reviewed the psychological and cultural obstacles to change not to argue that reform is impossible but to counter naïve assumptions about innovation and to assert that reform, if it is to succeed must accept the realities of human nature." (p. 51)

The implications of the Evans research for instructional leadership are twofold. First, improvement strategies must be designed around what is known about the school's culture of teaching. So, for example, if the culture of change has always been a bottom-up process, the instructional leader makes sure teachers are involved not only in the development of an improvement initiative, but in determining when an instructional improvement is needed. Second, the ability of an instructional leader to influence and inspire desired instructional change often depends on building relationships and increasing face-to-face communication. This means transforming the relational trust established with individuals into a culture of teaching that includes a collaborative commitment to a course of action and consistent practice. Teachers must feel like they have been genuinely involved.

"To learn about the culture you really need to be immersed in it. I found that talking with teachers and principals, observing in classrooms, doing demonstrations in classrooms and working with staff in professional development all helped me better understand the culture of teaching." ~ Anita

"I found out about the culture of teaching through individual conversations with teachers, students, and administrators; visiting classrooms, and presenting workshops that allowed me to establish relationships with the staff. The workshops promoted discourse that allowed me to learn more about how the participants/staff felt about teaching, learning, their students, and their supervisors." ~ Jay

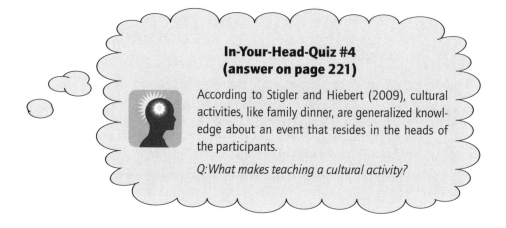

In-Your-Head-Quiz #4
(answer on page 221)

According to Stigler and Hiebert (2009), cultural activities, like family dinner, are generalized knowledge about an event that resides in the heads of the participants.

Q: What makes teaching a cultural activity?

JOURNAL REFLECTION

Before moving on to Chapter 4, Helping Teachers Learn More About Teaching, take time to write in your journal. Here are some suggestions for possible topics and subtopics to write about. Select the one that you believe will give you the most insights at this point in your work.

Beliefs About Student Learning

Do you think most of the teachers in your school possess the same belief system about how students learn best? __Yes __No

- Regardless of how you answered the question above, what are the implications for your work as an instructional leader?

Autonomy

Would you say that the majority of teachers in your school are autonomous when it comes to their choice of teaching methods? In other words, do they resist efforts to change how they teach? __Yes __No

- Regardless of how you answered the question above, what are the implications for your work as an instructional leader?

Culture of Teaching

In every school, there are certain aspects of the culture of teaching that both support and hinder desired instructional change.

- What would you say is the most striking aspect of your school's culture of teaching that supports desired instructional change? What could you do to leverage this dynamic to create better learning opportunities for students?
- What would you say is the most striking aspect of your school's culture of teaching that hinders desired instructional change? What first step could you take that might counteract this deterrent to desired instructional change?

Learning Opportunities for Students

Think of a recent lesson or episode of teaching that you have observed that you believe was a fine example of a learning opportunity for students.

- What made this learning opportunity so good?

TRY THIS: WHAT IS BEHIND THE METHOD?

Chapter 3 makes a distinction between methods and beliefs. Here is a chance to extend an understanding of that premise.

You look at teaching methods all the time, but do you really think about the beliefs that are behind those methods?

The best way to answer these questions is, of course, by visiting classrooms. To do this, however, you will need a plan.

(Continued)

(Continued)

So . . . try THIS:

- Make yourself a T-chart. On the left-hand side, write the heading "Methods," and on the right-hand side "Beliefs." Leave room for 20 visits.
- During a week, go into 20 classrooms at random, 10 minutes per visit.
- In each class that you go into, write down the method that is currently used by the teacher. For example, the students are doing seat work or the teacher is lecturing.
- Walk out of the classroom, but before you go into the next classroom, write down what you think the teacher's belief is about using the particular method that you saw. Just a simple belief statement will do.
- When you have done 20 classrooms, sit down with the data and ask yourself: What am I learning that will help me become a better instructional leader?

LEADERSHIP TEAM ACTIVITY

Analyze This

Purpose

Start with the end in mind.

- Discover how a school's culture of teaching impacts the work of an instructional leader.
- Use a collective analysis to better understand the challenges and to leverage strengths for continued instructional improvement.
- Visualize the action needed to transfer seminar learning and understanding to current instructional leadership practice.

Perspective

- Teachers and administrators are immersed in a culture of teaching. It is a complicated phenomenon that cannot be easily understood nor dismissed as the way things are. To be truly understood, the culture of teaching must be understood from different points of view.

Challenge

- To be effective, an instructional leader must dig around inside the culture of teaching, which sometimes can be a little hard to take. The challenge is to learn how to read the culture of teaching.

Plan

The basic steps for facilitating this single-focus seminar:

1. Prior to the seminar:
   a. Have everyone on the leadership team complete the "Analyzing the Culture of Teaching" (starts on page 53)
   b. Have the composite scores (anonymous) from each leader, for each of the 10 sections, placed in a matrix handout.
2. Provide time for a 60-minute seminar session with the leadership team.
   a. Go through the analysis together.
   b. Start identifying themes or patterns.
   c. Do the follow-up found on page 61.

Personal and Team Connections

- Participants will be asked to connect their unique leadership challenges to the content of the seminar.
- The team will ask two essential questions: (1) What have we been learning? (2) How can we use this learning to strengthen our work as instructional leaders?

BRIDGE TO CHAPTER 4

The logic of creating better learning opportunities for students needed to close the teaching gap might read something like this:

1. Student learning will not improve unless the learning opportunities for students improve.
2. The learning opportunities for students will not improve unless the teaching methods used to create them improve.
3. The teaching methods cannot improve unless the teachers learn more about teaching.
4. Therefore, it is paramount for instructional leaders to help *all* of the teachers learn more about teaching.

Creating better learning opportunities for students is a big challenge, no doubt about it. Teachers and instructional leaders who see themselves as 'educators' are hard at work every day helping students understand what they are learning and applying that learning in ways that are both practical and meaningful. They challenge students to think and to use their imaginations.

But even educators who understand how students learn best have to work in a culture of teaching. A school's culture of teaching is often complicated, making it a struggle to even implement desired instructional change. As Alfie Kohn (2010) points out, it means "putting kids before data" (p. 29). There are data for everything in education these days, but sometimes we forget why we need it.

In line with the research of Haberman (1991) on good teaching, in order for serious improvement to occur, all of the teachers—not just the individual teacher—must be the unit of change. One teacher getting better at teaching is good for some students; all teachers getting better at teaching is good for all students.

Working to improve teaching is like entering an empty railroad tunnel on foot. You want to get to the other side of the mountain, but you are not quite sure if there is a train coming or not. Unlike the railroad tunnel there is one thing about instructional improvement that you can always count on—the need to help teachers learn more about teaching. Stigler and Hiebert (2009) remind educators that teaching is something we can study and improve. This important premise leads us into the next chapter.

So, what is the best way to help teachers learn more about teaching? Common sense says that the answer to this question is in the classroom. After all, that is where the teaching and learning takes place. But, ironically the classroom is often the least likely place where teachers learn about teaching. Chapter 4 will take you through this *tunnel* of professional learning grounded by the firm belief that the classroom is where teachers (and instructional leaders) can (and should) learn the most about teaching. You will also see how teachers working together to solve problems of practice can learn more about teaching. Yes, there is light at the end of the tunnel. An effective instructional leader can help teachers learn more about teaching, and in so doing, close the teaching gap.

C H A P T E R   F O U R

Helping Teachers Learn More About Teaching

"Just as teaching is a cultural activity and difficult to change, teacher learning is also a cultural activity and thus subject to many of the same forces that keep traditional teaching practices in place."

—Stigler and Hiebert, 2009 (p. 182)

INTRODUCTION

Teaching is the number-one school-related factor for impacting student learning (Leithwood, Seashore Lewis, Anderson, & Wahlstrom, 2004). That is such an important research finding. It gives credibility to experience and common sense. But, unlike other professionals, most teachers rarely learn about teaching by observing in each other's classrooms. Teachers are more apt to learn about teaching through professional development and in-service workshops.

"The classroom is the practicum. That is where the real learning about teaching takes place." ~ Anthony

Not surprisingly, the 2009 *MetLife Survey of the American Teacher* (Harris Interactive) revealed that the majority of teachers and principals believe greater collaboration among teachers and school leaders would have a major impact on improving student achievement. It turns out that the least frequent type of collaborative activity is teachers observing each other in the classroom and providing feedback. The survey revealed that less than one-third of teachers or principals report that this frequently occurs at their school. The challenge for an instructional leader is how to inspire teachers to learn more about teaching, especially from each other's classrooms. When there is more attention paid to the teaching methods, the chances of reducing the teaching gap are greater.

Let me be clear. There is nothing wrong with workshops. If they are classroom-based and designed around the needs of students, they certainly can help teachers and education leaders improve their practices. But even excellent workshops are no match for the level of teacher learning available in classrooms. The value of teachers learning from their teaching is grounded by the emerging research of Gallimore, Ermeling, Saunders, and Goldenberg (2009) on school-based inquiry teams and the longitudinal research of Stigler and Hiebert (2009), which confirms their proposition that it is the teaching itself that is the best context for learning how to improve instruction. Experience teaches us that there is no greater challenge awaiting an instructional leader than trying to facilitate teachers learning more about teaching, especially as professional learning moves closer to the classroom.

Throughout this part of the book, you will be encouraged to rethink how teachers learn about teaching as you are introduced to ideas and strategies aimed at helping you overcome some of the major roadblocks to the study of teaching within a school setting. Teachers learning more about teaching are on the road to aligning beliefs and practice—the opposite of the teaching gap.

"The classroom is the only place that you can actually apply what you have learned and see if it works. I do think that staff development, extensive reading, and interaction with other teachers are very important for gleaning new ideas. But when it comes right down to it—you need to try it in the classroom, reflect on the results, and modify based on your knowledge of the students and the curriculum." ~ Anita

#3: There Is Madness in My Method

John Sullen is the Elementary Science Coordinator in a suburban school district. He was hired to help teachers in Grades 3–6 improve science teaching. John is a master science teacher and is considered by peers to be an expert in inquiry-based science instruction. John often does demonstration science lessons that the teachers and students enjoy very much. After the demonstrations, John urges the teachers to try the methods he has modeled. For the most part, elementary science in this district is taught in a traditional fashion using a variety of text resources, online programs, and multimedia.

For the past two years, all fourth-, fifth-, and sixth-grade students have had to take an end-of-year state test in science. The test consists of three parts: basic science facts, key concepts, and a laboratory experience. The one major concern was the district's poor showing on the inquiry-based laboratory experience.

John was called in to meet with the elementary administrative cabinet. They wanted his recommendations for improving the science test scores. John told the administrators that despite his efforts, most classroom teachers were still not comfortable teaching science. He felt the real sticking point was inquiry-based instruction. None of the teachers in Grades 3–6 had any experience with this approach to science learning.

Shortly after the administrative cabinet meeting, the Assistant Superintendent for Instruction called for the formation of a K–6 Science Committee with John as chair. The goal was to improve science achievement. There were two objectives that first summer:

1. Develop a Science Teaching Guide (STG) for Grades 3–6 with suggested teaching methods and resources.

2. Offer a special 2-week institute for inquiry-based science instruction. Two lead teachers from each 3–6 grade level in the six schools would participate in this hands-on learning experience.

Year 1:

- Lead classroom teachers worked with John to develop the Science Teaching Guide (STG), especially the inquiry-based methods. These teachers provided the pilot classrooms.
- Other teachers were invited to observe the pilot classrooms.
- A few nonlead teachers tried some of the new science teaching methods on their own.
- Science teaching changed very little for most teachers.
- Student performance in science remained about the same as the previous year.

Year 2:

- The summer institute was repeated.
- All teachers in Grades 3–6 were expected to begin using the STG.
- John was very busy going from classroom to classroom supporting teachers trying the new methods.
- Some teachers were excited about using inquiry-based instruction with their students.
- Some teachers were hesitant to try inquiry-based instruction.
- Student performance in science dipped a little bit, especially in the part 1 and 2 science facts and key concepts.

Year 3:

- The summer institute was repeated once again.
- John was doing some instructional coaching with teachers struggling to implement inquiry-based instruction.
- Science teaching was changing for many of the teachers.
- Student performance in science declined a little more in the part 1 and 2 science facts and key concepts. Students did much better on the inquiry-based laboratory experience.
- The seventh- and eighth-grade science teachers began complaining to their administrators that the incoming students

were not as well prepared for science as they had been in the past. Their factual knowledge and understanding of key science concepts were down from previous years. Was it because of these new teaching methods?

- Some of the elementary teachers were beginning to question the new methods. They talked about going back to the way they used to teach science. They said, "At least we will know what we are doing."

By the end of the third year, there was much confusion about elementary science education. Two camps had emerged: the teachers who believed in inquiry-based science instruction and the teachers who believed in the more traditional methods for teaching science. When in a room together, these teachers did not get along and there were instances where feelings were hurt. The matter was never resolved. Sometimes a method can lead to madness. This case is a good example of just that. As James Stigler (2010) writes:

Some methods are better than others. But because teaching is complex, often certain methods are better in certain situations. Thus, it is not enough just to improve the methods teachers use. We also need to improve teachers' capabilities for selecting the best method to use in each particular situation, and of implementing that method in an expert way. (p. 30)

This case illustration reinforces four important points:

1. The methods that a teacher uses are very personal.

2. The selection of teaching methods is in the professional domain of a teacher.
   - When an instructional leader sees the need to influence the selection of methods, the leader must also assume the responsibility for helping teachers to understand why and how.

3. When the selection of methods is different from those used in the past, teachers in the grade levels below and above the target grades must be involved at the start of the implementation process.

4. It is never an *all or nothing situation.*

    o The selection of teaching methods depends on the needs of the students and the skill of the teachers to know when and how to use those methods.

WHAT IS GOOD TEACHING?

This is the question that powers Chapter 4 and perhaps all of education these days. What is amazing is how few schools take the time to wrestle with this question. Maybe it is because educators take it for granted that everyone knows what good teaching is. Nothing could be farther from the truth. According to Vygotsky (1978), teaching involves the act of identifying what a child knows and can do within the Zone of Proximal Development (ZPD) and then providing the appropriate scaffolding (i.e., hints, prompts, cues, and strategies). The ZPD is the area between what a child can do independently and what he or she can do with assistance. The most effective instruction is aimed at each child's ZPD.

One person who has studied good teaching is Martin Haberman, and his work deserves special attention. In 1991, Dr. Haberman wrote a classic article in *Phi Delta Kappan* titled "The Pedagogy of Poverty Versus Good Teaching." Although Haberman's research was conducted in urban education, you may feel, as many do, that he has identified how most teachers teach today. His list of the teaching acts that constitute the core functions of urban teaching can quite easily be applied to all teaching:

• giving information • asking questions • giving directions • making assignments • monitoring seatwork • reviewing assignments • giving tests • reviewing tests	• assigning homework • reviewing homework • assigning questions to be answered using a search engine • settle disputes • punishing noncompliance • marking papers • giving grades

Haberman contends that this basic menu of teacher functions characterizes all levels and subjects. A primary teacher might give information by reading a story while a high school teacher might give information by reading a biology text. These acts of teaching have come to be recognized as "teaching." Students, parents, educators, business leaders, and politicians all consider these teaching acts to be teaching. But is it good teaching? To answer this important question, you may wish to use the Haberman article with teachers as a basis of discussion about what good teaching is.

"The principal should demonstrate effective teaching in every staff development activity that engages the teachers as students." ~ Anthony

SELECTING THE BEST TEACHING METHODS

One of the hallmarks of a master teacher is her ability to select the best teaching method for a particular situation or student need. Of course, a teacher cannot select the best teaching method without a variety of methods at hand. Selecting the right teaching method is a challenge. The classroom setting below might help to explain why.

A middle school social studies teacher is concerned that her students are not thinking deeply enough about the key concepts in their study of the American Revolution. The students' oral and written responses to textbook questions do not reflect the level of understanding the teacher expects. This *moment in teaching* helps to define the teacher's ability to select the best method for the situation. The teacher could just keep on teaching and implore her students to think harder. Or, she could show the students a few examples of the best written responses and ask them to think and write like that. But, this teacher knew the situation called for something more. She knew she had to formulate questions that foster student engagement and confidence and show her students how to answer those kinds of questions.

She started building confidence by modeling her own thinking out loud—showing students how she would respond to the same textbook questions. Next, the teacher wrote with the students using some of the strategies she had modeled. She invited the students to think together during a shared speaking and writing experience.

Finally, the students were given time and support to practice with new questions developed by the teacher. The results were dramatic. The students were speaking and writing with a greater depth of understanding. What made the difference?

Obviously, the difference is the teacher. Somewhere along her career, she had made incremental improvements to her teaching. She had expanded her knowledge of teaching methods, but what is even more important, the teacher knew when and how to modify her teaching approach. The social studies teacher did not have to wait for the data to arrive. The source of information she needed to select the best teaching method was right in front of her—her students. By listening to her students, talking with them, and reading their written responses, the teacher discovered that the situation called for a different method of teaching. She was able to put that assessment into action.

"I believe that teachers generally do what they know how to do—if they knew *how* to improve instruction, they would already be doing it." ~ Bill

There are three key implications for instructional leaders when it comes to helping teachers select the best teaching methods:

1. Helping teachers expand their knowledge of teaching methods (experience and inquiry)

Before doing anything, talk with the teachers about how they select teaching methods. What triggers them to change methods? Be sure there is a clear understanding about why teachers have to become proficient at selecting the best methods. Knowledge of teaching methods can be expanded around a common student need. It makes sense to teachers, and it has an immediate payoff. The instructional leader is the facilitator.

Teachers can expand their knowledge of teaching methods by starting with the methods currently in use. Due to teacher isolation, it is not surprising to discover one or more teaching methods that are unfamiliar to some of the teachers. Start with the known.

Once the currently in use methods are exhausted, the teachers can look at other teaching methods by communicating with teachers outside their school and by reviewing professional journals. Seldom do teachers work together to investigate teaching methods.

A blend of experience and research (e.g., Annenberg Institute, 1997) has shown that when teachers look at student work or watch a lesson episode together they are in a much better position to see the need for expanding teaching methods.

2. Helping teachers become better student observers (kid watchers)

Observations made during class time and by examining student work products can do more to inform teaching than anything else.

Students teach teachers. They challenge educators with their thinking as well as their behaviors. Students are the recipients of hundreds of hours of teaching. That makes students *outliers* of teaching and learning (i.e., outside normal experience).

Students, even first- and second-grade students, know the difference between a teaching method that helps them learn and a method that is boring. Tap into that knowledge the way a doctor monitors a patient's vital signs before revising treatment.

Start where the teachers are. What are they already doing? What do they want to learn next?

Here again, there is value in having a group of teachers watch the same media-driven lesson with time for follow-up discussion. Try to find a 10- to 20-minute relevant video that focuses on what the students are doing and saying. It is essential that the teachers are able to see and hear the students.

Interviewing students one-to-one or in small groups can quickly reveal misconceptions and misunderstandings about the concepts being taught in class. What teachers learn from students will impact their selection of teaching methods. Students might say that the teacher goes too fast or that they need to see more examples.

Ask someone (preferably a student) to videotape a teacher's classroom. The focus should be on what the students are doing and saying, not on the teacher. The teacher watches the tape (alone or with colleagues) listening and watching for *diagnostics* (clues or signs) that may signal the need for a different teaching method. Students might be experiencing difficulty with a homework assignment and need additional explanation.

"It is also useful for instructional leaders to co-teach classes so the teachers can observe their own students. What do they notice? What are the implications? After doing this, encourage teachers to consistently set aside time during instructional blocks for observation of students and to record notes about their observations. What are they learning from their students?" ~ Ardis

3. Helping teachers implement the best teaching method (technique into practice)

Even if you improve teachers' capabilities for selecting the best method, they still may have difficulty implementing those methods in their classrooms. This is where teachers will appreciate your help. Spend some time talking with teachers about implementing teaching methods. Have them identify what they have done in the past. What helped? What was difficult? Share these ideas with everyone involved in the discussion.

Ask teachers if they are currently working to implement a teaching method. For example, elementary teachers might be setting up learning stations. Middle and high school teachers might be trying to provide for the needs and interests of their students through small-group instruction or using a new lesson design.

Your work here is driven by invitation, and your role is much the same as that of a coach. Your assistance might be indirect (e.g., finding needed resources) or more direct such as assisting the teacher in the classroom when the teaching method is being introduced. Implementing the best teaching method sometimes requires substantial effort, on the part of the teacher, involving new teaching strategies and significant course restructuring. If this extends beyond your level of expertise, then your role is to locate a teacher(s) who has had experience putting a similar teaching method into practice.

"Be a source of inspiration/motivation when the staff struggles to improve instruction throughout the building." ~ Jay

MIRROR ON THEIR PRACTICE

"Mirror on their practice" is borrowed from an earlier quote by Ardis, one of the Voices of Experience. It is the essence of moving teacher learning closer to the classroom. Think of "mirror on their practice" whenever you think about helping teachers learn more about teaching. When teachers begin reflecting on what they are doing in the classroom, the improvement process is moving forward. Before teachers feel comfortable putting the "mirror on their practice," they may wish to put the mirror on someone else's practice. You may have already tried this next suggestion, but just in case, here it is.

Locate a short (15–20 minutes) lesson episode that you can show to a group of teachers. Be sure that the teacher in the lesson is not from your school and that the subject, grade level, and students are relevant for your teachers. The lesson you select does not have to be a fabulous lesson, but it does have to have credibility with the teachers.

Together with the teachers, develop a simple guide sheet for viewing the lesson. Pick something you and the teachers are interested in. For example, you and the teachers might decide that you are going to look at ways the teacher provides feedback to the students or the kinds of questions she asks. Remind the teachers to concentrate on the teaching, and not on the teacher. Discourage any attempt to evaluate the lesson. The goal is to use the lesson episode to stimulate a follow-up conversation about the value of teachers observing lessons and then discussing them together. Record everyone's ideas and see that they all get a copy.

Repeat this same activity at least once or twice more. Each time pick a different lesson and a different guide sheet. Consider ways to inspire teachers to observe each other's classrooms. Encourage them to pick some aspect of their teaching that they would like to learn more about. Invite the participating teachers to share their experience when the group meets again.

Keep a written summary of what they say, and make sure everyone gets a copy of it. You do this because the summaries provide a focal point for future staff meetings and a valuable record of experience for teachers to read over and reflect on with respect to their own teaching.

"I believe the classroom is the best place to *practice* improving teaching—to try new ideas and to make adjustments in meeting the needs of students." ~ Bill

PEER REVIEW OF TEACHING

Peer review of teaching refers to the participation of teachers in the development of teaching methods. In this context, peer review is not about colleagues evaluating each other's teaching. Rather, it is about teachers who engage in similar teaching activities that are willing to share content expertise and specialized skills to improve student learning. The case below serves as an introduction into the realm of teachers developing teaching methods together.

#4: Moment in Teaching

The sixth-grade teachers in a large rural school district were concerned that their students were having difficulty understanding the physical, social, and historical characteristics of world communities. Part of the reason involved geography. Many students were having a hard time using geography skills such as observation, map reading and interpretation, classification, and organization. Geography skills were an integral part of the social studies curriculum, and it was apparent they had not been emphasized in the earlier grades.

When the sixth-grade teachers met to discuss the situation, they soon discovered how little they knew about their own teaching of geography. The teachers decided that the first step should be to learn more from each other about teaching geography. The sixth-grade chair suggested a peer review of teaching focused on geography. The teachers liked the idea and broke up into groups of two or three. They used a rotating substitute teacher to provide time for peer visits and follow-up discussions.

After several months, the teachers met to discuss their findings. Teaching strategies in use included connecting students with personal experiences, textbooks, and printed material and the use of interactive computer software and other multimedia devices. The teachers agreed that they were good strategies for teaching geography skills. What was missing was the amount of time being spent on teaching them. They had their plan of action.

Here again is the strength of teachers learning together from their own work as teachers. Strange as it may sound, teachers rarely take the time to learn from each other, which confirms the long-held notion that the work of most teachers is hidden from colleagues. The opportunity for shared learning is denied. But there are ways to break up this isolation.

PEER OBSERVATIONS

Independent peer observations occur when teachers, on their own, watch each other teach and discuss what they are learning. Nowhere is an understanding of the culture of teaching more important than when it comes to facilitating independent peer observations, and ironically, nowhere can teachers learn more about teaching than by watching each other's lessons and discussing them together. High on the list of activities for classroom-based study of teaching are independent peer observations.

It would seem that a natural progression from viewing taped teaching episodes, looking at student work products, and participating in lesson study would be teachers learning in each other's classrooms. But, as you know from your own experience, this is not always the case. You may be privileged to work in a school where teachers observe each other teaching on a regular basis, but for most instructional leaders, peer observations are the exception, not the rule.

With this in mind, one of the best times to open the doors, so to speak, is when teachers are looking for answers to an instructional problem or are trying a new teaching approach or method. Since perception is greatly influenced by context, we need only return to Case Illustration #2 (page 41) to see that the teachers implementing strategy instruction were in the best position to learn from each other. Teachers are far less likely to resist peer observations when they are absolutely convinced that the focus is on the methods, not the teacher.

Even the most confident and motivated teachers can become edgy about peer observations if their concerns about time and their questions about purpose are not adequately addressed. As noted earlier, release time is often the culprit for getting staff together during the teaching day, but it is not the only issue when it comes to facilitating peer observations. Unless teachers have figured out a way to observe each other on their own (which is the ultimate level of peer observations), any attempt by school leaders to encourage this practice may be met with resistance.

The obvious course of action for instructional leaders wishing to encourage and facilitate independent peer observations is to start slowly. That means knowing and building on the comfort zone of individual teachers, recognizing past experiences (positive and negative), and most importantly thinking of how you can make it easier for teachers to be in each other's classrooms. But, remember, in the end, teachers must believe there are sound reasons for wanting to participate in peer observations. If they do not believe that watching each other teach is valuable—well, you can finish this sentence.

The other side of the peer observation equation is how teachers make use of what they are learning by observing each other's classroom lessons. The real potential of this practice is found in the discussions teachers have about what they have been learning from each other. The instructional leadership goal is for teachers to be able to conduct productive discussions on their own. You can facilitate this high-level professional interaction in a number of specific ways:

- Make it possible for teachers to find the time not only to watch each other teach, but to conduct the important postlesson discussions (debriefing). Without some release time, all is lost.
- Become part of a small group of teachers who are trying peer observations. Your role is as a teacher, a neutral observer, and a participant observer in the follow-up discussions. Learn with the teachers.
- Provide teachers with a few ideas on how they might learn from each other. The key here is to make sure that the discussions generated by peer observations do not become merely collaborative patronizing sessions. They must be focused on student needs and instructional improvements, not just to tell each other how great they are.
- Help teachers put the emphasis on what the students were doing during the lessons observed. The questions then become: How could our teaching more effectively help students learn? What do we need to do in order to improve?
- Encourage teachers to keep a record of what they are learning from each other and offer to provide the means for distributing this *action research*. Over a period of time, this

information will more than reinforce the value from independent peer observations and will serve to encourage more teachers to get involved.

TEACHER-LED TEACHING CIRCLES

Teaching circles have generally been associated with college or university teaching (e.g., Harvard has used them for years), but they are just as effective for K–12 teachers. A teaching circle is made up of a small group of teachers who share common concerns and interests related to teaching. They meet on a regular basis to generate and share ideas, offer resolutions to teaching problems, and act as advisors to one another. The focus of the discussions in a teaching circle is always on improving teaching methods.

The teachers in a teaching circle could be from the same department or grade level or an interdisciplinary group. The latter has proven to generate richer discussions and sidesteps the rehashing of familiar ongoing issues that can bog a group down. The key to the success of teaching circles is that they are voluntary, teacher led, and centered on teaching. For obvious reasons, this is one school-based group that administrators should not join. Topics of discussion can be as varied as the backgrounds of the participants. Below are a few possible topics for teaching circles in Grades K–12:

- Asking higher level questions
- How to facilitate learning centers
- Designing the bridge to a lesson
- What can we learn from looking at student work together?
- How can I keep instructional groups flexible and challenging for students?
- Is it a good idea to establish a behavior management system?
- How to engage students in large group settings
- "Will this be on the test?"
- How to implement small-group work in class
- How to use strategy instruction in the core academic areas
- Using technology and other instructional media
- Discussing and implementing one's vision of learning

A good time to introduce the idea of teaching circles is when a group of teachers are interested in some aspect of their teaching, such as teaching mini-lessons. You can help the teachers get started by helping one of the teachers to learn how to facilitate the first teaching circle. A simple agenda for teaching circles provides the basis for facilitator training.

Discussion Topics

- The facilitator could give a few examples
- Ideas from the rest of the teaching circle group
- Focus on the concrete rather than the abstract
- Meetings
- Doable (e.g., once a month for 45 minutes)
- Keeping meetings interesting with value to teaching
- Worthwhile use of time
- Meeting format
- Breakfast, lunch, after school
- Common planning period
- Ground rules?
- Guest speaker (optional)
- Different perspective or expertise
- Do not sacrifice the informal, casual, idea generating discussion
- Membership (decided by the group)
- Open to any teacher
- For a particular department or grade level
- Adapting and changing

The benefits of teacher-led discussion groups include increased communication among teachers, exchange of ideas and teaching approaches, enhanced collegiality and professionalism, and an opportunity for teachers and staff new to a department or grade level to learn more about the school's instructional program. Teaching circles give teachers a risk-free way to improve teaching and solve problems of practice. The role of the instructional leader is to provide support and guidance and to be there for the teachers when they decide it is time to turn discussions into actions.

TEACHER-LED LESSON STUDY

Lesson study was first introduced in Chapter 1 as one process that is fully consistent with Stigler and Hiebert's six principles for improving teaching. The practice of lesson study originated in Japan and is a proven way for teachers to create better learning opportunities for students (Lewis, 2000; Stigler & Hiebert, 1999; Takahashi, 2000; Takahashi & Yoshida, 2004). In simplest terms, lesson study is a process whereby teachers can systematically examine their own teaching practice and, in so doing, improve the effectiveness of the experiences they provide their students (i.e., better learning opportunities).

The success of a lesson study is measured in teachers' learning, not in the perfection of a lesson. That better lessons are created is a secondary by-product of the process but not its primary goal. Groups of teachers work to formulate lessons that are taught, observed, discussed, and defined. Teachers engage in lesson study only a couple of times a year because the process is intense.

If you need further information about conducting a teacher-led lesson study, visit the website of the Lesson Study Research Group at http://www.tc.edu/lessonstudy/lessonstudy.html. This site has helpful background information (two examples shown below) and detailed procedures and resources for moving forward with this teacher-led professional development process.

- Lesson study is practiced in every content area from language arts, to math, and even gym. Lesson study provides a process for teachers to examine their practice in order to answer questions about how they can serve their students more effectively, and this can be done in all subject and grade levels.
- Lesson study is practiced as a school-based activity as well as in groups that come together across schools. In a single school, lesson study often brings together teachers from all grade levels and different areas of interest. This diversity of participants is seen as providing a rich perspective to lesson study activities. (Lesson Study Research Group, 2010, "Facts About Lesson Study")

Implications for Instructional Leaders

There are some challenges for conducting a lesson study that should be considered before trying this approach to creating better learning opportunities for students. Below are some suggestions for addressing the instructional leadership challenges related to facilitating lesson study:

> *Providing the time.* Lesson study is time intensive and requires a considerable amount of advanced planning and coordination. If possible, start with a small group of teachers who share a common planning time or teachers who have the fewest number of scheduling conflicts during their instructional day.
>
> *Focusing the study lesson.* Choosing the right goal and related research question is absolutely essential in order for lesson study to be of value to the students and the teachers. Once a group of teachers commits to lesson study they must establish the focus.
>
> *Teaching the study lesson.* Selecting the person to teach the study lesson could be as simple as someone volunteering or the teachers agreeing to take turns. It usually depends on the experience of the team and the relationships they have with each other. The fact that the lesson is developed collaboratively and the focus is on the teaching methods, not the teacher, is usually enough to alleviate the fear of teaching in front of one's peers.
>
> *Establishing guidelines for debriefing.* The team should decide on the final guidelines for debriefing a study lesson. It is advisable to start with an established protocol (e.g., from the Lesson Study Research Group) and to make any changes or additions that the members of the study team feel are necessary.
>
> *Selecting the facilitator.* A good facilitator can make a big difference to the success of a lesson study debriefing, especially if the process is fairly new to everyone in the group. If possible, try to find a person who has had some experience as a facilitator or who has been through lesson study as a teacher.

TEACHER-LED LEARNING AND IMPROVEMENT

Despite all of the attention and rhetoric directed toward collaboration these days, most teachers continue to work in isolation. Research from Leonard and Leonard (2002), summarized below, may help to explain why teachers find it difficult to work together in meaningful job-embedded ways.

PROBLEMS OF COLLABORATIVE PRACTICE

1. Teachers do not consider their schools to sufficiently exhibit expectations of or support for regular, high levels of collaborative involvement.

2. Teacher work continues to be characterized by competition and individualism and lacks the type of trusting, caring environment that is more conducive to collaborative practice.

3. There needs to be greater articulation of underlying values and beliefs about educational practice that is tempered with respect for diverse professional opinions and practices.

4. Teachers are dissatisfied with scheduling and appropriations of time, which often serve to deter collaborative practice.

5. Teachers need professional development directed at improving their collaborative skills.

But, wait, there is hope. In an article written by a fourth-grade teacher, titled "When Teachers Drive Their Learning" (Semadeni, 2009), the author tells about his school in Wyoming ". . . which provides time during contract hours to study best practices in that area, and then rewards that teacher for improving his or her teaching skills. In this model, teachers collaborate to study, experiment, and coach one another in research-based strategies. School climate surveys show that teachers have higher morale and more willingness to work together to solve difficult problems since they adopted this method of teacher learning" (pp. 68–69).

Couple this frontline teacher's voice with two important research-based findings about working with teacher-driven improvement teams and there is even more reason to be optimistic about overcoming the problems of collaborative practice.

Finding #1:"Teachers need both conventional professional development to deepen their pedagogical content knowledge as well as a stable inquiry and learning setting in which to convert that knowledge into better lessons and practices" (Gallimore, Ermeling, Saunders, & Goldenberg, 2009, p. 14).

Finding #2: "Time for collaboration by itself, even when administratively supported, is unlikely to improve achievement unless additional conditions are in place that structure its use. Those conditions are leadership and protocol" (Saunders, Goldenberg, & Gallimore, 2009, p. 23).

In an effort to move teacher learning closer to practice, well-intentioned instructional leaders can offer what Gallimore and colleagues (2009) call "critical learning opportunities." According to these researchers, "Critical learning opportunities arise when teachers and staff focus on a specific student need over a period of time and shift to an emphasis on figuring out a solution (instructional and otherwise) that produces a detectable improvement. This is not just trying out a variety of instructional activities or improvement strategies. They hypothesized that these critical learning opportunities would draw teachers attention to and help them discover causal connections between their teaching and student performance" (p. 8).

For example, a team of fifth-grade teachers questioned whether their students had the skills needed to demonstrate comprehension through written responses. The team worked on this *investigation* during an entire school year. They tried a number of strategies (e.g., showing students samples of well-written responses to comprehension questions) and discovered that they could take a tough learning problem and break it down into smaller manageable parts. They were successful and so were the students.

Inquiry-Based Protocol

Saunders and colleagues (2009) suggest that there are two ingredients necessary for teachers to learn more about teaching and solve instructional problems: (1) a workable inquiry-based protocol and (2) leadership. The protocol that follows is from their work with grade-level learning teams and offers instructional leaders a way to help teachers make better use of their time together (p. 23).

The team will:

1. Identify a specific and common student need to work on together.

2. Formulate a clear objective for the common need.

3. Identify a promising focus (instructional or otherwise) to address the common need.

4. Decide on one necessary preparation to try the focus in the classroom or elsewhere.

5. Try the team's focus in the classroom or elsewhere.

6. Analyze student work or behavior to see if the objective is being met and evaluate the outcome(s).

7. Reassess: Continue and repeat cycle or move on to another area of student need.

Before continuing, it is must be said that real progress is being made learning how to help teachers move the learning of teaching closer to practice. The research-based work of Gallimore, Saunders, and others bears watching, as it holds great promise for instructional leaders determined to learn how to facilitate effective teacher learning teams. The more you understand about how to help teachers study teaching collaboratively, the farther along your school will be in closing the teaching gap and creating better learning opportunities for students. You can learn more about teacher-led learning teams by reading "Five keys to Effective Teacher Learning Teams" by Gallimore and Ermeling (2010).

"Encourage teachers to visit each others' classrooms. Teachers can learn so much from each other and the opportunity to observe learners." ~Ardis

In-Your-Head-Quiz #5
(answer on page 221)

- Lawyers learn more about how to practice court law by observing other lawyers in court rooms.
- Nurses learn more about nursing by working in hospital rooms with other nurses.
- Surgeons learn more about surgery by observing other surgeons in operating rooms.

Q: But how do most teachers learn more about teaching?

JOURNAL REFLECTION

The *not so hidden* purpose of Chapter 4 is to convince you that John Dewey (1965) was right when he said, "Intensive, focused opportunity to experiment with aspects of practice and then learn from that experience" was the way that teaching should be improved. Before moving on to Chapter 5, take time to write in your journal. Here are some suggestions for possible topics and subtopics to write about. Select the one that you believe will give you the most insights at this point in your work.

Method Madness

If you have encountered a situation where teachers in one particular grade level are being asked to use methods that are not familiar to the teachers in the grade levels above and below, you may wish to respond to the following questions:

- How did the leaders (you and others) handle this situation?
- What were the results?
- What is the lesson to be learned?

Responsibility, Not Buy-In

There is a difference between teachers taking responsibility for results and mere buy-in (i.e., superficial commitment to someone else's idea or practice).

- If you were trying to influence teachers to consider peer review of teaching methods or peer-to-peer observations, what is the evidence that the teachers were taking responsibility for leading these two types of collaborative activities?

Cultural Connection

Suppose you discovered that the culture in your school was deterring collaborative practice. Competition, individualism, and lack of a trusting environment were squelching most attempts at authentic teamwork.

- How would you approach this situation?
- Whom would you involve?
- What would your first goal be?

Professional Communities

Some professional communities enforce traditional methods of teaching while other professional communities develop innovative methods of instruction. Look around your school, what types of professional communities do you see?

- What are the implications for your work as an instructional leader?

TRY THIS: PRACTICE WHAT YOU PREACH

Chapter 4 is all about helping teachers learn more about teaching, especially from the classroom. But that is no simple task!

You know that many teachers are reluctant to observe in each other's classrooms, but have you ever experienced what that feels like?

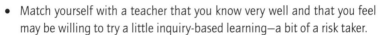

If not, try THIS:

- Match yourself with a teacher that you know very well and that you feel may be willing to try a little inquiry-based learning—a bit of a risk taker.
- Ask the teacher if you could come into his or her class and teach a 30-minute lesson that the teacher was planning to teach her or himself. Not a canned lesson—please!
- After planning with the teacher, develop your lesson the way you think it should be taught.
- Ask the teacher to watch your lesson and to give you some targeted feedback that will help you do a better job next time. That is the key to this inquiry!
- Meet with the teacher and listen to what he or she has to say.
- Ask the teacher if she or he learned anything from watching you teach.

Think about what you learned from this experience that may help you to better facilitate teachers' learning more about teaching from each other.

TRY THIS: ASK TEACHERS

Chapter 4 offers a rather unique structure for instructional leaders when it comes to helping teachers select the best teaching methods.

(Continued)

(Continued)

It is rare that instructional leaders ever spend quality time talking with teachers about their teaching methods (e.g., how they select new methods, observe students, and implement changes).

So rare, in fact, that you may wish to wish to give it a try.

If so, try THIS:

- First, familiarize yourself with the three implications for instructional leaders, which begin in the book on page 76.
- Select two highly effective teachers that you believe would be willing to sit down together (the three of you) to discuss how they select their teaching methods.
- Keep the discussion simple, taking notes about each of the three questions below:

  1. How do they expand their knowledge of teaching methods?
  2. How do observations of your students influence your choice of teaching methods? Can you give examples?
  3. Once you have decided to use a different teaching method how do you go about implementing that change?

What you learn from this rich discussion with highly effective teachers will make you a wiser instructional leader when it comes to helping less competent teachers select better teaching methods.

 LEADERSHIP TEAM ACTIVITY

Appreciative Inquiry

Purpose

Start with the end in mind.

- The leadership team will work together to discover new ways to help teachers learn more about teaching from the classroom and each other.
- Visualize the action needed to transfer seminar learning and understanding to current instructional leadership practice.

Perspective

- Unlike many other professions, teaching continues to be pretty much an isolated profession. Even today, many teachers still work mainly in their own classrooms and rarely, if ever, observe in the classrooms of their colleagues. Why is that?

Challenge

- To be effective, an instructional leader must constantly strive to better understand the barriers to improving teaching and learning. One such barrier is teacher isolation, that is, teachers working alone in their classrooms.

Plan

The basic steps for facilitating this single-focus seminar and follow-up:

1. Provide time for a 60-minute seminar session with the leadership team and a follow-up session a week later.

2. Have everyone complete the following T-chart:

   a. Left-hand side: What keeps teachers from wanting another teacher in their room while they are teaching?

   b. Right-hand side: What keeps teachers from wanting to be in another teacher's room as an observer?

3. Follow-up

   a. Ask each leader to repeat this same perceptual activity with the teachers in their school, grade level, or department.

   b. Meet again to discuss the findings.

   c. Compile all T-charts and distribute to each team member.

Personal and Team Connections

- Participants will be asked to connect their unique leadership challenges to the content of the seminar.
- The team will ask two essential questions: (1) What have we been learning? (2) How can we use this learning to strengthen our work as instructional leaders?

BRIDGE TO CHAPTER 5

As you leave this chapter, take the words of Stigler and Thompson (2009) with you, "Improving the very methods that teachers use— has the unique potential to lead to sustainable improvements that can be built on by each subsequent generation of teachers" (p. 443). What a powerful statement. It serves as a reminder that your work as an instructional leader is so important.

Helping teachers learn more about teaching is the way forward to closing the teaching gap. No program, policy, or reform initiative can replace what teachers need to learn about improving their methods of teaching. The means to an end are emerging, and there are good choices available from peer observations to lesson study. But, keep in mind, to be effective, teacher learning must be teacher led. This means that instructional leaders must help teachers assume greater responsibility for improving teaching and support them in their efforts to try.

The next chapter is about how to successfully lead the change needed to improve the methods that teachers use. This is the heavy lifting. You will see how developing a theory of action perspective can help you to not only lead desired instructional change, but to involve teachers in the development of needed instructional change. You will learn more about how to lead change perceived to be second-order in nature (i.e., beyond the realm of current competencies), including how to deal with resistance to change. But, perhaps most importantly, you will learn how to help teachers change methods where students are not succeeding. That is the goal of good teaching.

As you begin, ask yourself this question: With all the pressure surrounding school improvement in recent years, has the teaching really changed that much? Your answer to this question will help you to find a perspective for taking a closer look at leading instructional change.

C H A P T E R   F I V E

Successfully Leading Instructional Change

"Student achievement will not improve unless and until we create schools and districts where all educators are learning how to significantly improve their skills as teachers and as instructional leaders."

—Wagner et al., 2006 (p. 23)

INTRODUCTION

It seems like everyone is clamoring for change these days. The 21st-century folks want to prepare kids for the global economy while the back-to-basics bunch wants students to learn the old-fashioned way. Meanwhile, many instructional leaders, teachers, and administrators work in schools where they feel pressure everyday to increase student achievement. Get those scores up!

Suppose Mick Fleetwood had started a band called Fleetwood Educators instead of Fleetwood Mac. The lyric line in his signature song, "Winds of Change" (1974), might have been written as: "The winds of instructional change won't blow away." If you are an instructional leader, the message is clear—the need for instructional change does not go away. The pressure an instructional leader feels navigating the *winds of instructional change,* whether desired or mandated, is real. For many instructional leaders, the winds of instructional change are probably more accurately described as a hurricane coming right at you. But, like all hurricanes, no two are exactly alike. To be successful, the best instructional leaders develop new perspectives and mind-sets. Past success is no guarantee. Sometimes past success even gets in the way as educators cling to what has worked before rather than striving to make needed improvements.

One of the basic tenets of this book is that good leaders inspire people to change. As an instructional leader, you are a key ingredient in the change process. Successful instructional leaders understand the mechanics of change. They modify their leadership responsibilities and practices in accordance with the magnitude of change. Most importantly, they are able to effectively work through the human side of change. Successful instructional leaders understand the dynamics involved and use sound judgment when dealing with resistance. They have the best chance at closing the teaching gap.

This chapter will help you to meet the ongoing challenge of leading instructional change. Remember, to be successful, you may need to make a few changes yourself. The goal is to turn your hurricane into a zephyr. The case illustration below provides a realistic perspective for better understanding the complexities of leading desired instructional change. The case puts a new face on the old adage that "the more things change, the more they stay the same." That saying, unfortunately, holds an important fact of experience with respect to the gap in teaching.

 ### #5: When the Rug Gets Pulled Out

Annemarie Costello is an experienced middle school social studies teacher and has been an assistant principal for 3 years. The building leadership team consists of the principal, another assistant principal, and five teacher leaders who teach only three periods a day. Annemarie was assigned by the principal to lead instructional improvement while the other assistant principal manages scheduling, student activities, home/school relationships, and discipline. Annemarie's responsibilities include working with the teacher leaders as part of an Instructional Leadership Team (ILT). There are 875 students in Grades 6–8 (50% African American, 40% Caucasian, and 10% Hispanic). Nearly 65% of the total student population receives a free or reduced-price lunch.

For three consecutive years, the reading comprehension scores (from district and statewide tests) for all three grade levels declined. An analysis of formative and summative assessments revealed that many students were experiencing difficulty comprehending non-fiction reading, especially in mathematics, social studies, and science. Students lacked the skills to make inferences needed to draw conclusions; determine importance; summarize passages in their own words; compare and contrast ideas, concepts, and vital information; and support opinions with facts and evidence from the text. The teachers were seeing the same deficiencies in the students' daily work.

The mathematics, social studies, and science teachers taught lessons that were mostly teacher centered and traditional in nature. For years, using these very same methods, the core academic teachers had excellent results in terms of student success, but the new state tests were demanding higher level skills—skills many of their students seemed to be lacking. The mathematics, social studies, and science teachers readily admitted that they were not literacy teachers and expected their students to come to them with basic reading and writing skills. They believed that these skills were best taught in the elementary grades and in the middle school English Language Arts classes.

Annemarie decided over the summer that improving reading comprehension would be the number-one goal in the middle school improvement plan. In September, together with the District's Director of Reading, she co-facilitated a data-driven meeting with the ILT. The purpose of this meeting was to create a sense of urgency about need to improve reading comprehension.

Annemarie and the ILT looked at several possible options, but decided to go with a comprehensive professional development plan that included four 2-hour workshops along with ongoing follow-up classroom support. The goal was to help all of the core academic teachers learn how to integrate strategy instruction into their teaching (e.g., Reciprocal Teaching and Question-Answer Relationship). The teachers would have to be able to help students become more self-directed learners with the ability to monitor and adjust their approaches to learning. The principal was in total agreement with the ILT's plan of action.

Annemarie met with the core academic teachers in September so she and the members of the ILT could present their improvement plan. The meeting went well. There were only a few questions raised by the teachers. It appeared that the staff was prepared to meet this challenge head on and do whatever it would take to put strategy instruction into practice.

By the end of October, all of the core academic teachers were knee deep in the professional development program and were learning many effective strategies for improving reading comprehension. Annemarie was busy making sure that the professional development was going well and that the teachers involved felt supported as they began implementing new practice. Things continued this way throughout November and December.

After the holiday recess, Annemarie began hearing "rumblings" that things were not going well with the strategy instruction initiative. The ILT teacher leaders reported that many of the core academic teachers were feeling pressured and felt they were spending far too much class time teaching reading strategies. They were worried that they were falling behind with the pacing of their curriculums.

Many of the teachers complained that they had not been involved in the decision to implement strategy instruction. By the end of January, the core academic teachers were so frustrated they requested a meeting with the principal to express their concerns.

It would be the rare instructional leader who has never had the rug pulled out from under her, especially when trying to lead change. Sure, what happened to Annemarie and her ILT might have been avoided if the staff had been involved from the beginning, but that is not the point. The point is that leading change, in particular change that takes staff out of their teaching comfort zone, requires adjustments in leadership responsibilities and practices. You are the key ingredient for working with teachers to change methods where students are not succeeding. So get on your rug and let us see if we can keep it under you.

The first part of this journey deals with the distance between beliefs and actions. To be fair, it is not easy for a teacher, or an instructional leader for that matter, to put their beliefs into practice. It is important, however, to raise those beliefs to the conscious level on a regular basis. It is the start of a personal accountability system that asks the question: Am I doing what I say I believe? Spending more time with ineffective teaching methods is not the answer.

"Sitting in classrooms and talking with teachers allows an instructional leader to learn what is valued in this community of learners." ~ Ardis

ALIGNING PRACTICE AND BELIEFS

Picture this. You walk into a school, and in the front hall you see a poster titled "Our Beliefs About Student Learning." You stop to read the first belief statement on the poster. It says, "We believe that students cannot be given understanding; it has to be constructed so students can see for themselves the power of an idea for making sense of things." Excited by the possibilities that this belief about self-discovery conjures up in your mind, you continue walking down the hallway, stopping in as many classrooms as you can along the way. At first, you just brush it off to bad timing, but in classroom after classroom, you see the same thing: students sitting at their desks, looking bored, and copying notes that have been posted on a SMART Board. This is not what you were expecting to see.

As an instructional leader, you no doubt have run across situations where you see differences between the school's belief system about learning and what is happening in the classrooms. This mismatch between beliefs and practice can even be found in schools that have received national recognition for excellence. Break out the antacid tablets!

An assertion put forth by Argyris (1991) may help you better understand the rationale for such a mismatch. "Put simply, people consistently act inconsistently; unaware of the contradiction between their espoused theory and their theory-in-use, between the way they think they are acting and the way they really act" (p. 7). Using this line of reasoning, it is safe to say that in the school example above the inconsistency was between the way teachers thought they were teaching and the way students were really taught. Keep this point in mind as you proceed through the chapter, as it is a key factor in explaining a teacher's defensiveness about their practice in the classroom.

"Conversations with teachers helped me develop a sense of my own style and how I needed to adjust it to better meet the needs of different staff members." ~ Bill

KNOWING DOES NOT ALWAYS MEAN DOING

"Advocates of 21st century skills favor student-centered methods—for example problem-based learning and project-based learning—that allow students to collaborate, work on authentic problems, and engage with the community. These approaches are widely acclaimed and can be found in any pedagogical methods textbook; teachers know about them and believe they're effective. And yet, teachers don't use them. Recent data show that most instructional time is composed of seatwork and whole-class instruction led by the teacher" (National Institute of Child Health and Human Development Early Child Care Research Network, 2005, p. 306).

CHANGING METHODS WHERE STUDENTS ARE NOT SUCCEEDING

The best teachers know a great deal about students. The best instructional leaders know a great deal about teachers. Below are some important considerations to keep in mind when you work with teachers to change methods.

Touching someone's teaching is very personal. In the culture of teaching found in most U.S. schools, teachers feel strongly about the selection of methods and prefer professional autonomy in their classrooms. Instructional leaders can never disregard the methods teachers are currently using, even if those methods are not helping students to succeed or are not providing the best learning opportunities. This dynamic will be discussed in more detail in the section on teacher resistance. Some teachers develop their own methods. They prefer to create strategies based on the needs of their students. Seldom do they seek outside assistance. Their teaching methods are their own. You could call these teachers *self-directed.* They believe teaching methods must be learner centered.

Self-directed teachers have no qualms about changing methods when they feel there is a need to do so. Self-directed teachers see flexibility as a means for teaching uninterested students. Get to know these *productive loners* well because they can be either be change agents or passive resisters.

Some teachers find it difficult to develop their own methods. They prefer to implement best practices and actively seek ideas from colleagues and teachers' manuals. They depend a great deal on outside resources. These teachers believe the methods they are using are the ones that work best for them. Know these teachers well as they often are the ones who resist desired instructional change.

Then there are many teachers whose methods fall somewhere between self-directed and dependent. This group of teachers makes up the majority. The important thing to understand here is that you need to know as much as you can about the teaching methods used in your school or district. It is not a question of right or wrong methods, as there are many effective teaching methods. It is a question of knowing the teaching methods in practice so you can more effectively *work with* teachers to change methods where students *are not succeeding.*

"To be more helpful an instructional leader needs to know the style, characteristics, strengths and weaknesses and effectiveness of every teacher in the school." ~ Anthony

The Transitional Practice Table below shows habits of practice that make it difficult for some teachers to modify or change their approach to teaching. Read the boxes until you come to a description that fits a teacher(s) you work with. Think about what you have done or might consider doing to help them change. Try it with several other teachers.

Elementary teachers who favor skills-based math instruction may find it difficult to transition to a developmental approach that emphasizes concepts, explanation, and knowing why.	Teachers who usually ask knowledge or understanding questions may find it difficult to transition to a method that requires asking students synthesizing or evaluation questions.
Science teachers who provide conditions for inquiry-based learning may find it difficult to transition to a method that uses scripted, programmed lab exercises.	Teachers who use multimedia to stimulate creative thinking may find it difficult to transition to a method rooted in commercially prepared computer programs and presentations.
Reading teachers who use basal readers and controlled vocabulary lists may find it difficult to transition to a method that involves shared and guided reading and literature circles.	Social studies teachers who teach primarily with lectures and the textbook may find it difficult to transition to a method that incorporates authentic learning projects and self-discovery.
Foreign language teachers who teach definitions with vocabulary books and quizzes may find it difficult to transition to a conversational method that immerses students in the second language.	English teachers who let students write about whatever interests them may find it difficult to transition to a method that has students respond to prompts and contrived situations.
Teachers who usually teach to the whole class may find it difficult to transition to methods that use cooperative learning or small-group instruction.	Teachers who are used to taking their students on a variety of nearby study trips may find it difficult to transition to an approach that uses only Internet-based "field trips."
Teachers who teach for understanding (e.g., students being able to explain and find evidence) may find it difficult to transition to programs that stress memorization to cover course material.	Teachers who facilitate learning by allowing students to struggle with new concepts and ideas may find it difficult to transition to a method that uses a more structured approach to new learning.

Primary teachers who are anchored in developmental learning may find it difficult to transition to mandated programs that are scripted or from a publisher's series.	Primary teachers who give children many worksheets to do may find it difficult to transition to a developmental program based on the needs of individual students.

If the world were perfect, working with teachers to modify or change methods where students are not succeeding would be a snap. After student needs are identified, instructional leaders and teachers would come together to pinpoint the deficiencies, take a look at current approaches and methods, decide whether or not there is a need for modifying or changing those methods, research the best methods or alternatives, develop a plan for moving forward, implement the plan, and carefully measure the results for any needed adjustments. Is your world perfect?

One of the best ways to learn from the *reality* of trying to change methods where students are not succeeding is by reflecting on your work. The aim of *deliberate* reflection (as opposed to random driving-in-the-car reflection) is to develop new perspectives and mind-sets to better inform your work with teachers. Below is a simple, in-your-head coaching activity intended to illustrate the value of guided reflection. It works better if you write down your response to each request for information. Give it a try.

First, think of your most pressing challenge as an instructional leader. Be sure that it involves the need to change teaching methods. Give it a name. For example: Helping high school teachers to establish learner-centered classroom environments.

Second, in one sentence describe the purpose of the change. For example: Instruction that begins with close attention to students' ideas, knowledge, skills, and attitudes to provide a foundation for new learning.

Third, list three things you did or are going to do to help lead this change. For example:

a. Have a team of teachers watch several high school lesson episodes from learner-centered classrooms and facilitate a follow-up discussion. Identify the strategies observed.
b. Facilitate a discussion about an article on learner-centered teaching. Identify a promising focus for moving forward

together such as attention to students' experience and background knowledge.

c. Working in pairs, have the teachers plan a lesson that begins by addressing students' experience and background knowledge. One teacher teaches the lesson while the other teacher observes. After discussing the lesson and making adjustments based on the first lesson, roles are reversed and the lesson is repeated. Each pair of teachers shares what they learned about learner-centered teaching at the next team meeting.

Fourth, identify an actual or predicted difficulty for teachers. For example: Teachers will feel they have lost the pacing of their lessons. How might you react to this difficulty? How would you support the teachers?

Before moving on, take a few minutes to bring closure to this metacognitive activity by responding to this question: What did you learn from this guided reflection that you can use as you lead instructional change in the future? Remember, when you reflect in writing you increase the opportunity to learn from your work.

"Provide time for teachers to analyze student work together and then share their ideas about how students learn and what instruction helps them to learn best and why." ~ Anita

DEVELOPING A "THEORY OF ACTION" PERSPECTIVE

"We have too many high sounding words, and too few actions that correspond with them."

—Abigail Adams, 1764

A theory of action perspective is the way a leader looks at moving from the current to the desired state in an organization. That is why it is so useful for instructional leaders trying to close the teaching gap. Although the perspective is best developed with input from others, the theory of action provides a level of accountability for the instructional leader. It answers the question: Is the instructional leader doing what he said he was going to do? With the help of a simple protocol, an instructional leader can write a theory of action to clarify the what, why, and how of any improvement initiative. If/then statements connect a leader's overall strategy to the actions and relationships critical to improved results.

The theory of action perspective comes from the organizational research of Donald Schön (1983). He discovered that it is possible for leaders of an organization to learn by simply reflecting critically upon their theory of action. Schön's significant work had important implications for educators. Unfortunately, few educators paid much attention. One who did was Tony Alvarado, long-time educational leader. He provided a good example of a leader's theory of action perspective during a presentation at the San Diego Summer Leadership Institute in 2005.

> My theory of action is—kids now are not learning, or large groups of kids are now not learning what they need to know and be able to do. It is teacher expertise—the knowledge and skill of teachers—that produces student learning. And so, if right now we have student learning that is not acceptable or good enough, then, in fact, what we need to do is improve the quality of teaching.

In the following table, there are three theories of action taken from coaching experience. They have been used successfully by school leaders to guide desired instructional change. In each example, the instructional leader developed a theory of action around a pressing student need. The instructional leader relied heavily on extensive collaboration with staff, classroom-based inquiry, and perseverance until the desired results were achieved. The three examples are presented in the same format that is used in this book to develop a theory of action.

Theory of Action #1: Elementary School Principal Reading Comprehension

Desired Instructional Change	Explanation of Why	Leader's Overall Strategy	If, Then Statement	Actions and Relationships
Improve the way we teach reading comprehension in Grades K–5	Beginning in third grade, our students experience difficulty comprehending their core academic subjects Skills like summarizing, drawing inferences, and making comparisons are lacking	Use collective inquiry to identify strengths of current teaching methods Build on those strengths Help teachers learn other methods Place greater emphasis on reading in the content areas	If the K–5 teachers and I focus on reading comprehension over an extended period of time, then we will figure out a solution that helps students better understand their core academic subjects	Create a collaborative inquiry-based relationship with teachers Provide the guidance and support needed for teachers to learn from each other Interview Grades 4–5 students (learn from them)

Theory of Action #2: Middle School Department Chair Problem-Solving

Desired Instructional Change	Explanation of Why	Leader's Overall Strategy	If, Then Statement	Actions & Relationships
Improve how we teach problem-solving	Students in Grades 6–8 have trouble solving Part 2 problems on the state tests. They need to become better problem-solvers	Concentrate on Part 2 learning Have teachers analyze their own data Talk with teachers about the *spiral effect* (revisit difficult concepts and skills over a longer period of time)	If I continue to stress the importance of spiraling missed or difficult topics, then the teachers in the department will make it a priority in their teaching	More collaboration with staff—get them on board Continue to work with regional math coach Provide better teaching opportunities Pop-in visitations with department staff Seek greater support from principal

Theory of Action #3: High School Assistant Principal Regents Exams

Desired Instructional Change	Explanation of Why	Leader's Overall Strategy	If, Then Statement	Actions & Relationships
To improve Regents exam results in Earth Science and Chemistry to a proficiency level of 80%	Level 1: Because student performance is below expectation Level 2: Because our students are not developing into the types of science students they can be Level 3: Break teachers' mental blocks about teaching and learning	Have teachers develop common formative assessments Have teachers begin mapping skills needed for success with regents	If I create the conditions whereby teachers realize there is a need to develop accurate formative assessments so the classroom is the testing environment, then student performance on summative exams will improve because the teachers will know before June 24 where the students are struggling	Help teachers plan together during the day Ask teachers to develop formative assessments by December 1 (provide guidance and support) Establish better instructional relationships with science teachers

To be effective, a theory of action must be thoroughly understood by everyone involved in the development process. If the contents of a theory of action are not clear, there is little hope that the anticipated actions and relationships can be realized. For this reason, it is wise to use a structured format like the protocol shown below. Use it to guide you through the development of your own Theory of Action. *You will need a Theory of Action to draw upon as you continue through this book.*

Desired Instructional Change	Explanation of Why	Leader's Overall Strategy	If, Then Statement	Actions & Relationships

Guiding Steps and Hints

First, think about a desired instructional change that you believe is needed in order to improve results for students.

- The desired change does not have to be a deficiency identified through student assessments.
- The desired change could be comprehensive and forward thinking—for example, the need to provide more authentic learning opportunities at all grade levels and within all subject areas.
- Talk about the proposed desired change during faculty, grade-level, or department meetings.
- No secrets; all professionals must have a chance to give their opinions.

The *why* is very important. Many initiatives lose their legs because too many teachers and leaders do not have a clear understanding of why they are doing something.

- The language of the *why* statement must be worked out carefully.
- Every word is important.
- There should be logical explanations that are both objective and subjective.
- The *why* must withstand tough scrutiny.

The leader's overall strategy means what you are going to do. It is not what the teachers are going to do.

- Here is a good example of a leader strategy: I am going to facilitate a series of inquiry-based discussions about the need to improve nonfiction writing.
- Here is a leader strategy that is not so good: The teachers will meet to discuss ideas for improving writing.

The if/then statement is the heart of your theory of action. They take a little practice to write before you will feel satisfied with how they sound.

- Be succinct. Make each word count.
- Don't copy someone else's statement. Use your own words.

Actions and relationships may be the hardest for you to develop, but don't leave them out. Think of them this way:

- You are not going to be able to tackle this change all by yourself.
- Actions mean just that—action.
  - What are you going to do and when?
  - Actions are why I refer to this process as leadership accountability. You make your actions public. The professionals around you can tell if you did what you said you would do.
- You may need to establish or strengthen relationships with other professionals.
  - Teacher leaders with teachers and administrators
  - Administrators with teachers and teacher leaders
- If you need to adjust relationships, specify what relationships.
  - Not going too fast
  - More listening
  - Problem-solving
- This last box is also where you may want to tell how you are going to adjust your leadership responsibilities. For instance:
  - More face-to-face communication with the staff
  - Stop hijacking teachers' time (team and individual)
  - Develop consistency in purpose and communication
  - Make sure there are other knowledgeable people, in addition to myself, who can answer questions and help address concerns

Unless you are developing a theory of action solely for yourself, the process is bound to generate questions and concerns from those involved. For instance, teachers will want to know *why* there is a need for a change or what they will specifically be expected to do. These are good questions and are better answered in the beginning than after the teachers have been directed to make a change. The whole idea of developing a theory of action is to make the desired instructional change visible to everyone with no surprises down the road. A theory of action serves as a source of leadership accountability.

A theory of action is usually measured in terms of improved teaching and learning. The process, procedures, and tools you use to determine results will vary depending on the desired change initiative. In today's world, data-driven reports receive most of the attention, but they are not the end-all for determining and reporting results. Remember, tests do not measure everything.

Perceptual information is critical to determining results in a people-based organization like a school. Besides the feedback from teachers and school leaders, listen carefully to the students. After all, they are the recipients of the teaching. Like patients in a hospital who influence health care improvements, students should be allowed to influence learning. The point is to listen.

"Students challenged my biases about learning and also challenged me to rethink the relationship between learners and learning." ~ Ardis

Developing a theory of action is a necessary beginning. It shows you are serious about inspiring needed change for better results. It is how you can be more accountable as an instructional leader. Think of a completed theory of action as your ticket for getting into the change game. But, as my second superintendent of schools used to say, "The proof is in the pudding." In the next section, you will get a chance to work on your pudding.

Please Note: If you have not yet developed your theory of action, please return to Developing a Theory of Action found on page 107. You will need a theory of action as you move through this section.

LEADING CHANGE PERCEIVED TO BE SECOND ORDER

This section deals with a level of change that is perceived to be second order in nature. That means that some teachers may feel that a desired instructional change is beyond their ability to implement. They believe it is easier to keep teaching the same old way. The case illustration below will serve as an introduction to this discussion.

#6: **Transforming a School**

James Poland is the principal of Lincoln Elementary School, located in a midsize metropolitan area. It is a neighborhood school with a diverse student body that numbers approximately 620 in Grades K–5.

The neighborhood is a mix of lower- and middle-class people, and like the rest of the country, the unemployment rate is up. Many of the teachers live in the community, and a few even went to the school as kids. Lincoln's scores on all state tests have consistently been average to above average when compared with other elementary schools. There is no middle school in the neighborhood, so parents of Lincoln graduates must choose from the eight middle schools spread out across the city. Follow-up studies conducted since 2004 indicate that the achievement levels of the students from Lincoln Elementary School either plateau or decline in Grades 6–8.

James, the faculty, and the parents' association have been concerned about Lincoln graduates for a number of years. Their efforts have included a thorough analysis of why Lincoln students cannot maintain or increase their level of performance through the middle grades. The results of this inquiry indicated that Lincoln graduates simply could not adjust to the demand for greater rigor expected in content-area subjects. Although Lincoln students were fluent readers, they lacked the higher level comprehension skills and strategies needed for greater understanding.

The dilemma facing James and the Lincoln Elementary School community pointed toward two possible solutions:

1. Change the K–5 instructional program.

2. Change the school so that it becomes a K–8 school.

Because money for reconstruction was not available, the parents, staff, and administrators at Lincoln Elementary School decided to change the instructional program at Lincoln across all grade levels.

After months of discussions, the Lincoln Elementary School community, under James's leadership, agreed to the following theory of action:

Since many of the students who leave Lincoln are experiencing difficulty with higher level learning, there is a need to modify the existing instructional program. Our theory of action is that if we can help our students develop improved skills and strategies, then they will be more successful in Grades 6–8.

James and the leadership team, which included the assistant principal and grade-level chairs, developed a course of action that included far-reaching professional learning and collaboration. Immediate attention was given to mapping higher level skills and strategies across each grade level.

At the end of the first year, the staff was exhausted and the parents were frustrated. Teachers grumbled that they were spending too much time in meetings and workshops. They were being asked to implement unfamiliar teaching methods. Some teachers said they were losing confidence in their teaching abilities.

Students, conversely, became more and more confused as they were expected to reach higher levels of understanding. The fun stuff in school seemed to be missing. They complained at home that the work was too hard. School was boring. A few children begged their parents to let them stay home.

There were times when James felt like he was on an island. Even his most positive building leaders were pushing back from this transformation. James wondered what had gone wrong and why?

Unfortunately, this case illustration is based on a true story. Despite the best intentions, the results were not good for students, teachers, parents, or administrators. You probably sensed some of the leadership problems as you read the case. James and the other school leaders did not comprehend the tremendous impact that school transformation would have on the entire Lincoln Elementary School community.

What this case illustrates is how important it is to know how a proposed change is perceived by those most closely involved. James and the other schools leaders seemed unaware of the magnitude of change that was inherent in the plan to transform the school. For a clearer understanding of that impact, please answer the questions from the table below:

Questions About a "Course of Action"	Yes	No
Do you think the "course of action" could have been implemented without significantly changing the instructional practices at the Lincoln Elementary School?		
Do you think the transformation was a logical and incremental extension of the instructional program that existed at the Lincoln Elementary School?		
Do you think the proposed instructional changes fit within the existing values and belief systems of most of the teachers at the Lincoln Elementary School?		
Do you think the "course of action" could be implemented with the knowledge and skills that existed among the teachers at the Lincoln Elementary School?		
Do you think the proposed instructional changes could be implemented with the resources that existed at the Lincoln Elementary School?		
Do you think there would be common agreement in the Lincoln Elementary School community that the "course of action" was necessary?		

The magnitude of change is in the eye of the beholder. It does not matter what the leaders think. What matters is how the change is perceived by staff, and in this case, by students and parents. Instructional leaders need to understand how intended change, even necessary change, is perceived by staff. Understanding the magnitude of change helps instructional leaders adjust their responsibilities and associated practices. For example, a second-order change often requires more face-to-face communication from leaders.

With the Lincoln case, if you responded with more "yes's" than "no's," then you perceive the plan for transformation as being what is termed a first-order change. For the vast majority of teachers and leaders, a first-order change is consistent with existing norms, values, skills, and knowledge. A good example of a first-order change is when the school hours are adjusted by 10 minutes. Most people barely notice the difference. This magnitude of change rarely requires a change or modification in leadership responsibilities.

If you responded with more "no's" than "yes's," then you perceive the plan for transformation as being a second-order change.

Second-order change is perceived as complex and is a break from the past. This magnitude of change conflicts with existing norms, values, skills, and knowledge. A good example of second-order change is when an elementary school switches from a basal reading program to a balanced literacy approach.

The magnitude of change in schools has definite implications for instructional leadership. Three practices for leading first-order changes—promoting cooperation, a sense of well-being, and cohesion among staff—may be all that is needed from a leader for successful implementation of such a change. For second-order changes, however, these three practices will be insufficient to fulfill a leader's responsibility. Here are two reasons why:

1. Second-order changes require leaders to work far more extensively with staff. It is possible that second-order changes will disrupt cooperation, a sense of well-being, and cohesion.

2. Second-order changes may confront group identities, change working relationships, challenge expertise and competencies, and throw people into stages of "conscious incompetence," none of which is conducive to cooperation, cohesion, and a sense of well-being.

The two statements above and the table that follows are based on the findings of the meta-analysis research reported in *Balanced Leadership: What 30 Years of Research Tells Us About the Effect of Leadership on Student Achievement* (Waters, Marzano, & McNulty, 2003).

Determining the Magnitude of Change

Although the magnitude of the change may be perceived differently by different people, it can be quite accurately predicted by using the two tables below. Knowing the magnitude of change (first or second order) is crucial to putting your theory of action into practice.

Change Perceived as First Order	*Change Perceived as Second Order*
An extension of the past	A break with the past
Within existing paradigms	Outside of existing paradigms
Consistent with prevailing norms, values	Conflicts with prevailing norms, values

Incremental	Complex
Linear	Nonlinear
Implemented with existing knowledge & skills	Requires new knowledge & skills
Implemented by experts	Implemented by stakeholders

Questions About a "Course of Action"	*Yes*	*No*
1. Can the "course of action" be implemented without significantly changing our instructional practices?		
2. Is the new work a logical and incremental extension of what we have done in the past?		
3. Does the new work fit within the existing instructional values and beliefs (paradigms) of the teachers?		
4. Can the "course of action" be implemented with the knowledge and skills that exists among the teachers?		
5. Can the new work be implemented with resources that are easily available?		
6. Will there be common agreement that the "course of action" is necessary?		

In-Your-Head-Quiz #6
(answer found on page 221)

According to the Mid-continent Research for Education and Learning (McREL), which one of the four leadership responsibilities listed below must be increased when leading change perceived to be second order?

1. Awareness of the personal aspects of staff

2. Communication with staff

3. Adapting leadership behavior to the needs of the situation

4. Knowledge about current curriculum, instruction, and assessment practices

Bill's reflection below may help you better understand how to lead change perceived as second order. Like so many other instructional leaders, Bill learned the hard way about leading desired instructional change.

"The situation that stands out in my mind took place in an elementary school when a core group of teachers and I initiated a study of alternative grouping options for our kids. It was my first attempt to bring about a second-order change. We ended up looking primarily at looping students and multi-age classrooms.

We took a whole year to study the options. We offered a college credit course on alternative structures; we had teams from multi-age schools come to staff meetings; we visited schools with alternative structures; we held parent meetings on various options; we brought parents from other schools to talk with our parents; we made a presentation to the board of education; we even had a "let's try it" week where we tried grouping students in multi-age grades.

The "we" was a core leadership team I put together to help with this effort. My sense through the whole process was that we were doing everything right. Looking back, I realize I was naïve and maybe blinded by the enthusiasm of the leadership team and the support of my immediate supervisor, the assistant superintendent.

What I neglected to notice (or chose to ignore) was that there was also a core group of teachers who were covertly opposed to the change. They attended the meetings and some of them even took the class but their reasons were more about gathering information to subvert the process.

They went to the superintendent and board members and rallied like-minded parents to undermine what the majority of the staff had voted to do. In the end, politics and political friendships won out. We opened the next school year with only two multi-age classrooms." ~ Bill

Bill's experience was a tough one. By his own admission, he failed to see what was really happening. Think of it this way, often there are two rivers that flow through the process of leading change perceived to be second order. The one you can see (above ground) and the one you cannot see (below ground). Ironically, it is not uncommon in situations like Bill's that the greatest advocates of change are often the greatest defenders of the status quo. For education leaders, the status quo is often the invisible barrier to closing the teaching gap.

RESISTING INSTRUCTIONAL CHANGE

 Not all change is powerful. Knight reminds education leaders that teachers may resist the need for instructional change if they do not believe the new practice will impact student learning. Teachers may feel they have been the *victims* of too many imposed changes in the past that have not benefitted students and have robbed them of valuable instructional time (Knight, 2009).

OVERCOMING RESISTANCE TO DESIRED INSTRUCTIONAL CHANGE

Knight's research offers a sound rationale for why teachers might resist the need for instructional change. As strange as it may sound, dealing with resistance to change is frequently a part of strengthening instruction. It is almost impossible to have one without the other. As an instructional leader, you can learn how to deal with resistance head on, or you can mourn the fact that not everyone sees the need for instructional change. The invented lament below provides a glimpse of resistance in action and will serve as a lead into learning more about how to overcome it.

Instructional Leader's Lament

(An adaptation of *A Mathematician's Lament*, Lockhart, 2009)

An instructional leader dozes off during a boring seminar and begins dreaming about school improvement. Maybe it was a nightmare, but it seemed so real. In her dream, she finds herself in a school where there are many school improvement initiatives underway. The mission statement says the goal is to maximize success for every student. Committees are meeting everywhere, shared decisions are being made, new programs are being implemented, workshops are being taken, and leadership teams are busy planning. Data of all kinds are posted throughout the building. Computer printouts with colorful graphs of student progress and achievement are on display for all to see.

Teachers and school leaders are so busy they can barely find time to see each other. Meetings pile up making it nearly impossible to do the work of teaching and leading. Students in the classrooms are working hard at their desks and tables. Many are using materials that will help prepare them for the tests ahead. The door to the staff room is open so the instructional leader peeks in. Most of the teachers are eating and talking.

Two of the inexperienced teachers seem excited about the new inquiry-based science curriculum. Over in the corner sit three teachers who look rather grumpy. She strains to hear their conversation. "Yeah, here we go again with a new science curriculum, just sit tight and this too will pass." Waking up in a cold sweat, the instructional leader realizes that it was just a crazy dream. She reassures herself that this could never be as she heads out to meet with the fifth-grade team.

On the school leader frustration meter, knowing how to deal with teachers who resist change is right up there with improving time management. This section has ideas that might help. For the sake of practical application, you need to think of a professional that you work with that you feel is the most opposed to change. Pick someone who consistently pushes back on almost everything you try to do, who avoids change like the plague. For the next few pages, this person will inform your learning. You know about data-driven education; well, think of this as resister-driven education. Call this person your "change fighter." You might as well learn from a master.

Build on what you know about your resister. What is one reason why you think this person opposes change? Fear of failure, creature of habit, no obvious need, and a closed mind are but a few reasons why some people have a tough time changing their mind-sets and behaviors. Think of something your change fighter does extremely well. For instance, he might have excellent organizational skills or maybe his questioning techniques are good. You have tried leveraging that strength for desired change but without much success.

Your theory of action is—if some teachers are resisting desired instructional change, their students may be missing better ways to learn. If I have a deeper understanding of the dynamics of human nature, then I will have a better chance to effectively work through the human side of change.

It bears repeating: Rule #1 about changing methods is to remember that touching someone's teaching is very personal. A teacher who is reluctant to make a desired instructional change may feel that the leader does not think she is a good teacher. Her reasoning becomes defensive as she constantly turns the focus away from her own behavior to that of others. For example, "I have not received enough support and time to do this."

It is well known that one of the factors that influence human behavior is change. According to Johnson (2008), "Significant change requires leadership that understands the dynamics of human nature. Resistance to change is an obstacle that needs to be openly addressed and properly negotiated" (p. 1). As mentioned earlier, in times of uncertainty, constant communication between the teachers and the instructional leader is essential. Teachers must see the need for the change and have a genuine role in the change process. Instructional leaders must accept and openly respond to the impact on human behavior inherent in the change process.

Suppose you have a situation where teachers are dragging their heels using the district's new framework for lesson planning. Before you meet with the teachers to discuss the matter, try an alternative approach to planning. Write a brief paragraph describing what you are going to do. Include what you plan to say and how the teachers would likely respond.

At the meeting, show the teachers your meeting scenario and give them a chance to react to it. In other words, let your planning document act as a catalyst for a courageous conversation. Keeping in mind that it takes at least two people to have a resistance; be prepared to hear some things about your leadership. What might your change fighter do or say at this kind of meeting?

Do not leave the meeting without trying to reach agreement about follow through. Keep it simple: What are you going to do? What are the teachers going to do? You and the teachers must have roles in the change process. Put it in writing after the meeting. Buy-in is not enough.

In the scenario just described, there was teacher buy-in. The teachers were a big part of developing the framework for lesson planning and had input all along the way. They received assistance with the framework for over a year. What was missing was responsibility. Responsibility is different from mere buy-in. When teachers assume responsibility for implementing something it means they will personally do whatever it takes to make it work. It also means they will accept the responsibility for the results—good and bad. They do not look for a way out.

Engage, Support, and Inspire

Using your change fighter as the individual to approach and the use of the framework for lesson planning as the context, work through the sequence below. Think of this as a dry run.

Engage

- Engaging your change fighter is the most delicate action.
- Choose the time and place carefully.
- Pick a time when you know the teacher will not be in a hurry to leave or just before he has to teach.
- The safest place for the change fighter to meet with you is in his classroom around his desk.
- Your attitude must be genuine. You want to help this person change.
- Think of how you will begin, but no notes. For example, you might say: "We have been using the framework for lesson planning for over a year now, where would you say you are in terms of putting it into practice?"

Support

- Identify how your change fighter defines support.
- Take your clue from him.
- Don't come to the meeting with a lot of predetermined strategies. For example, do not say: "Why don't you visit Tom next door? He has been finding success with the framework."
- Whatever your change fighter suggests for support, you must be willing to provide.

- If your change fighter says he does not want any support ask him "How do you plan to start using the framework?"
- In other words, you are providing pressure with support.

Inspire

- Inspiring the uninspired is not easy. It is difficult.
- To be motivated means to be moved to do something.
- How you choose to motivate/inspire your change fighter must be genuine.
- Sometimes kindness and patience inspires someone to try.
- Ask you change fighter who inspires his teaching. Maybe this person could help.
- Direct approach. For example, you could say to your change fighter, "What would it take to get you to use the framework for lesson planning?"

Your Change Fighter's Response	*Your Come Back*
• That I would be allowed to plan my lessons in my own way.	• Does your way include any of the components in the framework?
• Not to have to follow the framework step-by-step.	• I agree, how would you like to use the framework?
• Nothing. I just do not believe that the framework is right for me.	• Tell me more. I am interested in why you feel this way about the framework.

So what is the conclusion about overcoming resistance to change? You have to work on the human issues and not just the educational issues. You have to address the human issues openly with intent to be positive, but firm. You are the key ingredient in the formula for change.

STRENGTHENING INSTRUCTION

You would be hard-pressed to find a group of school leaders who do not want to improve instruction. Just stop for a moment and think about what is going on in your school with respect to the teaching and learning process. Is instruction on the front burner or the back burner?

Preceding sections of this book have dealt with a number of facets related to closing the teaching gap—creating better learning opportunities for students, leading change perceived to be second order, and selecting the best teaching methods. Each facet is aimed at strengthening instruction. This section takes a different angle and starts with a diagnostic tool for instructional leaders.

7 Disciplines for Strengthening Instruction

For more than 10 years, Tony Wagner and Robert Kegan have co-directed the Harvard Change Leadership Group (CLG). The CLG mission is to "create and gather knowledge to support sustained systemic changes in K–12 public education that results in improved learning for all students" (http://www.gse.harvard.edu/clg/index.html). One of the most useful resources ever to come out of the Harvard Change Leadership Group was their 7 Disciplines for Strengthening Instruction (Wagner, 2003).

The 7 Disciplines for Strengthening Instruction, found below, can be used as a diagnostic tool to help instructional leaders develop a shared understanding of what each discipline means for their school. "This diagnostic system of processes and intermediate goals is likely to contribute to the improvement of teaching and instructional leadership and, therefore, student achievement" (Wagner, 2004).

All members of the school or district's leadership team should complete the diagnostic by rating each statement across an implementation continuum. It is important to include evidence in the form of brief comments. Next, everyone in the group gets a chance to share his or her results. When all voices have been heard, each small group must develop a summary of results for each discipline. Finally, the entire group of school leaders (district, principal, assistant principal[s], and teacher leaders) should come together to exchange *what is* and *what needs to be.* This perceptual data should be posted and later sent to all school leaders for use with teachers.

The tool has added value when instructional leaders are asked to select one discipline that is a definite strength. Then they are asked how they would use that discipline to leverage the development of another discipline. For instance, if instructional leaders believe that one of their strengths is a widely shared vision of what good teaching is, they might use that discipline to improve staff meetings.

Diagnostic Use of the 7 Disciplines for Strengthening Instruction

Statement of Desired Instructional Change _____

7 Disciplines for Strengthening Instruction

1. The school/district creates understanding and urgency around improving *all* students' learning for teachers and community, and they regularly report on progress.

   ❑ Data are disaggregated and transparent to everyone.

   ❑ Qualitative (focus groups and interviews) as well as quantitative data are used to understand students' and recent graduates' experience of school.

   Not yet started   1   2   3   4   Well-established in our school/district

   Evidence:

2. There is a widely shared vision of what is good teaching that is focused on rigor, the quality of student engagement, and effective methods for personalizing learning for all students.

   ❑ Developed either by the school or by the district.

   Not yet started   1   2   3   4   Well-established in our school/district

   Evidence:

3. All adult meetings are about instruction and are models of good teaching.

   Not yet started   1   2   3   4   Well-established in our school/district

   Evidence:

4. There are well-defined standards and performance assessments for student work at all grade levels. Both teachers and students understand what quality work looks like, and there is consistency in standards of assessment.

Not yet started   1   2   3   4   Well-established in our school/district

Evidence:

5. Supervision is frequent, rigorous, and entirely focused on the improvement of instruction. It is done by people who know what good teaching looks like.

Not yet started   1   2   3   4   Well-established in our school/district

Evidence:

6. Professional development is primarily on-site, intensive, collaborative, and job-embedded and is designed and led by educators who model the best teaching and learning practices.

Not yet started   1   2   3   4   Well-established in our school/district

Evidence:

7. Data are used diagnostically at frequent intervals by teams of teachers to assess each student's learning and to identify the most effective teaching practices. Teams have time built into their schedules for this shared work.

Not yet started   1   2   3   4   Well-established in our school/district

Evidence:

Conclusions:
_____
_____
_____
_____

[Used by permission from Harvard Change Leadership Group]

When teacher leaders are part of this diagnostic process, they are in a better position to influence what needs to be done to strengthen instruction. When teachers as instructional leaders are left out of this process, their commitment to improvement may weaken. They may lack the motivation or the will to convince colleagues that something has to be done.

JOURNAL REFLECTION

Before moving on to Chapter 6, take time to write in your journal. Here are some suggestions for possible topics and subtopics to write about. Select the one that you believe will provide the greatest insights into your work now.

Successes teach

As you think about leading instructional change, what successes have you been experiencing?

- What have you been learning that will help you to be more successful leading instructional change in the future?

Mistakes teach more

Think of a mistake you made leading instructional change.

- What were you trying to accomplish?
- Why do you think it did not go well?
- What did you learn from this experience that will help you to be more successful leading instructional change in the future?

Change leadership must be shared

Write about a change challenge you have been working on.

- How have you modified your leadership responsibilities?
- Did the leadership adjustments make a difference?

Think of two people that you work with that could help you lead desired instructional change.

- Why did you select these two people?
- How could you approach them?
- What would you have them do first?

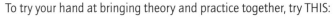

TRY THIS: BRINGING THEORY AND PRACTICE TOGETHER

Much of Chapter 5 is about the value of developing a "theory of action" to guide the why, what, and how of an instructional leaders work to successfully lead desired instructional change.

When developed and implemented properly, a "theory of action" can be a tremendous source of understanding for all teachers and administrators involved in an improvement initiative.

To try your hand at bringing theory and practice together, try THIS:

- Review the three "theories of action" found on page 106.
- Select an improvement initiative that you have either just begun or are planning to begin in the near future.
- Using the suggested format, follow the steps for developing a "theory of action" starting on page 108. Each component of the "theory of action" is described.
- Once you have completed your "theory of action," show it to someone who is either your supervisor, holds a position similar to yours, or is a person you consider to be a highly effective instructional leader.
- Do not tell this person anything about what you are doing, but rather, ask them if your "theory of action" makes sense? Could they follow it? Do they think teachers would benefit from this "theory of action"? How could they improve it?

 LEADERSHIP TEAM ACTIVITY

Leading Second Order Change

Purpose

Start with the end in mind.

- Members of the leadership team will help each other improve their ability to lead change perceived by staff to be second order in nature.

- Visualize the action needed to transfer seminar learning and understanding to current instructional leadership practice.

Perspective

- The fundamental changes sought in education are those that are the most challenging for teachers and administrators to embrace and implement. These improvements represent a second-order change that is perceived as such because the teaching and support required are not in the comfort zone of most of the educators involved.

Challenge

- To be effective, an instructional leader must be able to lead change perceived to be second order in nature. If not, educators are merely giving lip service to the need to improve teaching methods.

Plan

The basic steps for facilitating this single-focus seminar and follow-up:

1. Prior to the seminar

   a. Each member of the leadership team selects one teacher from the Transitional Practice table found on page 102. The selection is based on some prior experience working with this type of teacher.

   b. Each leader develops a list of the "action" they took to help this teacher change or modify their teaching and bring multiple copies to the seminar.

2. Provide time for a 60-minute seminar session with the leadership team.

   a. Each leader makes a 5-minute presentation about leading second-order change and gives the other members a copy.

3. The facilitator develops a matrix of instructional leadership strategies for leading second-order change.

   a. The team meets again to discuss the findings and to analyze instructional leadership responses.

(Continued)

(Continued)

Personal and Team Connections

- Participants will be asked to connect their unique leadership challenges to the content of the seminar.
- The team will ask two essential questions: (1) What have we been learning? (2) How can we use this learning to strengthen our work as instructional leaders?

BRIDGE TO CHAPTER 6

Closing the teaching gap often means successfully leading instructional change. For this reason, instructional leaders must not only be able to help teachers improve their methods (e.g., strategies, lessons, and assessments), they must also understand the human dynamics involved in the process (e.g., trust and cooperation), and be able to adjust their leadership responses appropriately. Without this type of "double-edged" instructional leadership, it is difficult to help teachers change methods where students are not succeeding. There is no question that the road to improving teaching and learning is bumpy. The potholes are sometimes called the status quo.

The road to improving teaching methods gets bumpier when the magnitude of change perceived by the teachers is second order in nature. You must be prepared to adjust and modify your responsibilities and practices in order to guide and support teachers struggling to regain the feeling of competence they once felt using a different method. You have also seen how a theory of action perspective can help teachers (and you) better understand the why behind the how as they become actively involved implementing a change initiative from beginning to end.

Keep in mind that your work as an instructional leader is the heart and soul of a school—improving the teaching and learning. For this reason, the best instructional leaders are constantly looking for ways to improve their effectiveness. They tend to read more professional journals, pay more attention to educational research, take advantage of more professional development opportunities, network with other instructional leaders, and above all, reflect on their work on a regular basis. The best instructional leaders practice what they preach when it comes to professional learning.

The next chapter is about you and what you can do to help yourself develop as an instructional leader. It opens the door wider on some conventional ways of motivating self-improvement and lets in a few new ideas that are not so well known. Starting with an up close and personal look at yourself, you will be invited to rethink how you communicate, inspire others to improve, and give and receive feedback critical for yourself and others.

This chapter also provides a final dose of reality regarding the circumstances that impact your work as an instructional leader. Finding your place in a complex system where the focus is often on data and accountability instead of on learning and teaching can be frustrating. Although most historians would say that education is always in a state of flux, there is no doubt that you are leading in a time of definite transition. How you reconcile yourself to this evolution will help define you as an educator and your work as an instructional leader.

CHAPTER SIX

Developing Yourself as an Instructional Leader

"I know that no matter where you are in your leadership development, this development never ends."

—Cohen, 2010 (p. 1)

This chapter will help you better understand why leadership development never ends. You may recall that one of the eight tenets essential for growth as an instructional leader is establishing a reflective practice. The case illustration below may be one of the best ways to demonstrate just how important it is for an instructional leader to learn on the job. Experiential learning is high on the list for self-improvement. A reflective practitioner thinks about her work and is often able to make needed leadership adjustments based on earlier reflections. As you will see, mistakes are a big part of those reflections.

#7: The Story of an Instructional Leader

Mary Beth Delgado is the assistant principal of the K–8 Green School, a job she has had for 2 years. She is in charge of the school's Instructional Leadership Team. There are two instructional goals for the Green School in the District's School Improvement Plan (SIP).

Goal #1:   That the school be taken off the state's School Under Registration Review list (SURR) by the end of the current school year.

Goal #2:   Develop students who can use their literacy skills and strategies (thinking, listening, reading, writing, and speaking) to maximize academic learning.

The leaders in the district office talk a lot about data-driven decisions and results. Mary Beth feels the pressure for accomplishing the School Improvement Goals. Her evaluation by the principal and superintendent is based, in part, on student achievement. Results on standardized tests, principal observations, and student accomplishments found in authentic learning projects form the basis of her performance evaluation criteria. Mary Beth's greatest challenge, and the one that keeps her up at night, is deciding how to approach the two School Improvement Goals. With so many improvement options available, such as the establishment of a professional learning community, instructional coaches, and classroom-based professional learning, Mary Beth cannot decide how she wants to move forward. She is thankful for having a supportive principal and teachers who get along well together.

Mary Beth is smart enough to know that all instructional improvement must pass through the classroom. She knows that it is the quality of teaching that will ultimately make the difference for students. The question that nags at her is: How should I go about improving the quality of teaching?

There are times when Mary Beth feels like she is trying to make improvements all by herself. She feels this way when she hears the superintendent compare the Green School with the other K–8 schools in the district. She feels this way at administrative meetings where instruction is almost never discussed. She feels this way when talking with her principal because he seems to have distanced himself from instructional matters.

Mary Beth sometimes feels she is working alone even when she is meeting with the teacher leaders. She feels this way because although the teacher leaders are concerned about declining student performance, most of them balk at the mere mention of substantial change. They worry that a desired change in practice will upset the teachers at their grade level.

Mary Beth knows that she made some mistakes in the past—mistakes that may be contributing to her frustrations about how to tackle the two school goals. Like the time, in her first year as assistant principal, when she was so enthusiastic about cooperative learning. She involved the Grade 5–8 teachers in deciding to embrace cooperative learning and then rushed them through a series of workshops. Little real change came from that professional development experience as teacher after teacher found cooperative learning too difficult to implement. With so many classes dedicated to subject areas and a bulging curriculum, teachers did not feel they had the time to devote to cooperative learning.

Then there was last year, Mary Beth organized a very successful Saturday morning tutorial program to boost student achievement. Things were going along smoothly until the classroom teachers discovered that the reading and math tutors hired for the Saturday morning program were using methods that were different from those being used in the regular program. Students became confused and parents registered complaints. The program finally had to be discontinued.

Anyone who is serious about improving teaching and learning will, at some time or another, feel the frustrations that Mary Beth felt. It is just the nature of the work. But, please take note of one simple fact: there is no big "S" on your chest. You do not need to be a Superwoman or a Superman to become a better instructional leader. You just need to want to learn.

INTRODUCTION

As a wise man once said, "He who knows others is learned; he who knows himself is wise" (Lao-tzu, *Tao Te Ching*). Perhaps that was the inspiration for Pete Townshend when he composed the hit song "Who Are You" in 1978. It is also the inspiration in this book for developing yourself as an instructional leader. Who you are is at the core of your being as an instructional leader. Knowing yourself is the foundation of helping others. It is what the kids mean when they say, "Where are you coming from?"

It is said that in the last years of his life, Michelangelo scribbled "ancora imparo" ("still, I am learning") in the margin of one of his sketches. He was 84 years old. The message was written (perhaps) in celebration of lifelong learning. Educators who embrace the philosophy of "ancora imparo" consider themselves first and foremost as learners.

Developing as an instructional leader is best learned through work informed by experience, feedback, research, and ongoing reflection as a practitioner. The purpose of this book has been centered on using these four beliefs about self-improvement. If you take advantage of the opportunities that your work allows you to grow, you will indeed grow as an instructional leader.

Peter Drucker (2006) wrote that "effectiveness can be learned." He believed leaders could help themselves to become more effective. Think of a time when you did just that—learned to be more effective. It could have been when you were more receptive to what others were saying or when you forced yourself to learn something new. As an educator, you know that students can help themselves improve more than anyone else. As an instructional leader, you must never forget that principle. As the saying goes, "Refine the skills needed to fuel your passion."

Unless of course you prefer to follow the lead of TV character, Michael Scott from the television show "The Office." When asked for the title of the book he was writing, he replied, "It is called *I'm Michael Scott—Somehow I Manage.*"

WHO AM I?

"History's great achievers—a Napoleon, a da Vinci, a Mozart—have always managed themselves. That, in large measure, is what makes them great achievers. But, they are rare exceptions, so unusual both in their talents and their accomplishments as to be considered outside the boundaries of ordinary human existence. Now, most of us, even those of us with modest endowments, will have to learn to manage ourselves. We will have to learn to develop ourselves" (Drucker, 1999, p. 2). Drucker's classic article titled "Managing Oneself" (Drucker, 1999) will give you valuable insights into your development as an instructional leader. The *Harvard Business Review* considers this article to be one of the best articles it has ever published. Thousands of leaders have used this article to energize self-improvement. It is readily available online. You are encouraged to read it.

Drucker uses five key questions to frame his commentary:

1. "What are my strengths?"

2. "How do I work?"

3. "What are my values?"

4. "Where do I belong?"

5. "What can I contribute?"

The point here is that you need to take every opportunity you can to know yourself better. It is the filament inside your instructional leadership bulb. Let it shine. Further along in this chapter, you will be reminded that feedback from others can help you learn more about yourself as an instructional leader. It is what Drucker (1999) meant when he concluded that, "The implication of managing oneself is clear: Only when you operate from a combination of your strengths and self-knowledge can you achieve true—and lasting—excellence" (p. 1).

CONNECT, NOT JUST COMMUNICATE

Knowing how well you communicate is an essential part of your self-knowledge. There are probably times when you feel that you are as much a communicator as you are an educator. Day after day, you are communicating with staff, teachers, leaders, students, and parents. You can barely walk down a hallway without having to stop and answer a question, explain something, remind someone about something, or just say "hello." But, in the words of George Bernard Shaw, "The single biggest problem in communication is the illusion that it has taken place." When do you believe you are at your best communicating? Here is a checklist to aid your thinking.* Check five statements below that you strongly agree with. I am at my best communicating when I:

1. __ Email everyone working on an improvement project.

2. __ Am leading a large group.

3. __ Have to explain something

4. __ Ask someone how things are going.

5. __ Post an important message in the staff room.

6. __ Listen without thinking of what I am going to say next.

7. __ Tell teachers and staff to stop in my office anytime.

8. __ Sit down with a teacher in her classroom and talk about what she is doing.

9. __ Am on the telephone, cellphone, or smartphone.

10. __ Use Skype or video conferencing.

11. __ Conduct a postconference.

12. __ Send and receive text messages.

13. __ Am leading a small group.

14. __ When I ask questions.

15. __ Write a good meeting summary or follow-up memorandum.

16. __Am on Facebook or Twitter.

Think about the five statements you checked. Why do you think you picked those five statements? Communication cannot be determined solely by your level of comfort or style. The instructional leader who is a good talker but rarely sends out timely hard copy information will leave a void of understanding and many unanswered questions and misconceptions. In the

*Although this checklist was designed to help you assess yourself as a communicator, you may wish to ask those around you for their feedback.

rapidly changing world of technology, one of your most important communication decisions is whether to communicate in
person. A good way to decide is to remember how you feel about
communication.

The emergence of collaborative school cultures, with their
shared decision-making, school-based planning, and Wiki Space
discussion boards, has accelerated the need to communicate
quickly and often. Communication overload is a problem in
practically every district and school. Professionals are spending
far too many hours sifting through emails, text messages, voice
mail, handwritten notes, and whatever messaging device is on
the horizon. It is what Leonhirth (2010) meant when he said,
"The challenge in the United States in the 21st century is not
how to find access to communication media, but how to escape
from them" (p. 1).

The paradox in all of this, however, is that despite all the
advancements with communication devices, people seem less able
to communicate on a personal basis. Ask yourself: "What kind of
communication do teachers need and expect when I am working
with them to change methods where students are not succeeding?" If you take nothing else from this section, believe that personal contact is the most important aspect of your instructional
leadership communication. Without face-to-face contact, you
may have the illusion that communication has taken place,
when in fact it has not.

Students, teachers, fellow leaders, and parents process communication from and with you based on their own individual perspectives and reality. Think of perspectives and reality like you
would a flour sifter. Its purpose is to separate wanted elements
from unwanted material. The farther you move away from personal face-to-face communication the more likely your message or
ideas will be sifted—and not always in ways you intended.
Connect, not just communicate.

"Conversations with teachers helped me develop a sense of
my own style and how I needed to adjust it to better meet
the needs of different staff members." ~ Bill

PERSUADING AND INSPIRING

Unless you own the school or are a person of mean disposition, you probably cannot order teachers to improve their teaching methods. You have to persuade or inspire them to improve. This is what is often referred to as the art of leadership. Persuading others is usually direct and intentional. The instructional leader may even say, "I am trying to persuade you to make better use of your classroom computers." The "power of persuasion" is well known. What is not so well known is how to do it better. Think about how you try to convince or motivate people. What works for you?

The chance of successfully persuading others is improved when the instructional leader understands what is really going on behind the scenes. Obviously, you would have a hard time convincing teachers to make better use of technology if they were experiencing frequent technical problems. But sometimes the subtext of resistance is not so obvious.

You may need to dig a little deeper before deciding whether the time is right to persuade. Sometimes waiting is the best strategy. Teachers respond better to persuasion when they are allowed to exercise some level of control or choice. Dean Rusk, Secretary of State from 1961 to 1969, offered a great suggestion, "One of the best ways to persuade people is with your ears—by listening to them." The method of persuasion can make a difference as the following example demonstrates.

Teachers in a rural school could not be convinced that having students keep learning logs would help improve learning. After listening to their reasons, the principal gave the teachers the option of trying learning logs for one semester with one of their classes. At the end of the first semester, these teachers were so excited about the benefits of learning logs they decided to use them with some of their other classes. After 1 year, there were only a few teachers on the sidelines. The actions of the first teachers who tried learning logs influenced their fellow teachers.

Inspiring

Inspiring someone is personalized motivation. A teacher may be inspired by an instructional leader simply because the teacher considers the instructional leader to be genuine.

Hanging inspirational posters in your office will not do the trick. It is your personal investment with those around you that will inspire them to improve or embrace desired improvement.

In one school, student performance in mathematics was steadily declining. The principal had done everything she could think of to improve student achievement, including having some tough conversations with the teachers. But the scores continued to decline. It turns out that the missing ingredient in this situation was the principal's inability to inspire her teachers. She could lead them, but she could not inspire them to change. The foundation needed to support personalized motivation had never been established.

The ability to inspire is often dependent on how you are perceived as an instructional leader. Helping yourself sometimes means seeking honest feedback from those who will level with you. Be like the old cowboy who once said, "If you're riding ahead of the herd, take a look back every now and again to see if they are still with ya." Connect, not just communicate.

GIVING AND RECEIVING FEEDBACK

Dr. Johnson was an English professor at a small state teachers college. About the second week of the first semester, he would assign each of his freshman classes their first essay. He would always ask his students to write about their hometowns. After the papers were corrected, Dr. Johnson would stand in front of each freshman class and hold up a fistful of their essays. Then, with the precision of a relief pitcher in baseball, Dr. Johnson would throw the papers at his students saying, "if you are going to write like this you might just as well go back home to your mothers."

The story above is true. You may have had a similar experience during your first year in college. College professors used (and perhaps they still do) this shock therapy strategy to let first-year students know that their writing needed to improve. Dr. Johnson's feedback to his tenderfoot scholars was dramatic, but it did not help them improve their writing. They needed more specifics.

Instructional leaders have a responsibility to provide feedback to teachers that will help them to improve their teaching methods and consequently student learning. Feedback can play an essential role in accomplishing that responsibility. But, as you know, giving teachers and staff constructive feedback is a lot like trying to sew a button on a custard pie. It is easy to push the needle through, but the thread will not hold. What follows next are two tips for giving constructive feedback. You will notice that they are all based on an instructional leader's knowledge of good teaching. If there is one secret to giving better feedback, it is being specific about the teaching. Anything less will be of little use to teachers.

Giving Constructive Feedback to Teachers

Constructive feedback is used to build things up, not tear things down. Teachers value constructive feedback when it helps them to clarify what they need to do or think about in order to improve. Targeted feedback guides further practice. Firsthand, practical experience has provided a few lessons for instructional leaders who wish to improve their ability to provide constructive feedback.

Whenever possible, start by validating some aspect of good teaching that you observed and do it as specifically as possible. For example, rather than saying the students were engaged, you might say: "The students completed the three activities that were part of the geography lesson. The students used the guide sheets to help them be successful."

Let the teacher know that you recognize effective aspects of their teaching. You might say something like: "I noticed that you were encouraging students to ask questions of each other. You were helping them to see that they can learn from each other by sharing ideas and asking questions."

Suppose you observed a teacher having difficulty managing small-group instruction. Make it clear to the teacher that small-group instruction is what you would like to discuss. You might say: "Today, I would like to talk with you about small-group instruction and in particular, ways that you can learn how to manage it more effectively." Provide examples from your observations that demonstrate this difficulty and seek input from the teacher before making your suggestions.

Here is perhaps the gold standard for giving feedback to teachers from Robert Marzano (2009): "Frequent feedback to teachers is beneficial if it accurately reflects the complexity of teaching and learning. Most importantly, supervisors must know their pedagogy. Content knowledge is great, but if you don't know pedagogy, you won't get the full complexity of teaching and learning, and you run the risk of giving bad feedback." This is sound advice for improving your feedback to teachers.

To a classroom teacher, the full complexity of teaching and learning may mean that someone understands their teaching in its entirety. The teacher believes that an observer understands what she is trying to accomplish, what her students are like, what she has been doing prior to this lesson or activity, and what is coming next. In other words, the observer sees the big picture. When a teacher senses this level of understanding in the feedback he or she receives, defense mechanisms are lowered. The teacher is more open to suggestions and recommendations for improvement. It is your understanding of teaching and learning that determines the quality of your feedback to teachers.

Observational feedback that circumvents the complexity of teaching and learning does not sit well with most teachers. They will consider the feedback to be somewhat superficial and perhaps think that the instructional leader does not know what he or she is talking about. When this happens, the door to possible improvement (via feedback) begins to swing shut.

Constructive feedback must be based on a teacher's own merits, style, delivery, assessment, and everything else connected to his or her teaching. It cannot be based on how you or someone else would teach the lesson or present the activity. Changing the focal point of the feedback can be a source of teacher resistance and resentment. One last point: If feedback is either always positive or always negative, teachers will distrust the feedback and it will become useless rather than constructive.

Receiving Constructive Feedback

As the saying goes, "What is good for the goose is good for the gander." With regard to feedback, that saying is relevant. You cannot improve as an instructional leader without honest, constructive feedback anymore than teachers can improve without feedback regarding their teaching. Receiving constructive feedback can be tricky. One of the chief problems about feedback is getting honest feedback. If you are lucky, you will be working with a few teachers or staff members with the courage to talk with you about your work one-on-one. Although this is somewhat rare, it does happen. This kind of candid constructive feedback is precious because it gives you a chance to clarify the points being made.

Surveys have been used by leaders for years to gather feedback from staff. The problem with many of these instruments is that they tend to be too general and do not inspire confidence that they are totally confidential. An alternative is to develop your own survey. Below are some points to keep in mind if you decide to develop one.

1. Make sure the survey covers specific aspects of your work as an instructional leader such as knowledge of teaching and learning, analyzing student information, developing lessons and assessments, building relationships with teachers, solving problems (instructional and human), facilitating better meetings, improving communication, and managing time.

2. Ask the teachers how you could make the survey as confidential as possible. There are online survey programs that are confidential. Two that seems to work well are http://freeonlinesurveys .com and http://surveymonkey.com.

3. Align the survey with your major instructional leadership responsibilities. For example, working on the School Improvement Plan or evaluating an instructional program.

4. Always give respondents an opened-ended question, such as: What suggestions do you have that will help me improve as an instructional leader?

Can You Take Constructive Criticism?

One of the hardest things in the world is to accept criticism, especially when it is not presented in a constructive way. Like mistakes, however, constructive criticism can be a most valued teacher. In fact, one of the reasons that some leaders do not grow on the job is because they shy away from constructive criticism. It is only when you know how others perceive what you have been doing that you are able to address your shortcomings. Criticism can be a tough pill to swallow, but it will help you to improve more than flattery. Adjust your expectations accordingly, believing, as former Secretary of State Dean Rusk once said, "Feedback is indeed the breakfast of champions." Connect, not just communicate.

REACTING TO ASSESSMENTS AND STANDARDS-BASED ACCOUNTABILITY

All around you there are politicians, corporate leaders, state educators, teachers, administrators, school board members, and parents who believe that by *setting the bar higher*, student achievement will improve. Does raising the bar in track and field help an athlete jump higher? Does measuring a child more often help the child to grow faster? The answer to these two questions is obviously "no." Yet one-size-fits-all assessments combined with the high stakes, standards-based accountability system created by the passage of the No Child Left Behind and the extension of Race to the Top Acts continue to dominate every aspect of American schooling. This juxtaposition of assessments and accountability systems influence how students are taught and how they learn in most schools. As an instructional leader, you have some tough choices to make in the pressure cooker world of education.

The National Center on Education and Economy released a report that may help you with your choices. It is called *An Assessment System for the United States: Why Not Build on the Best?* (Tucker, 2010). The report contains 11 research-based assessment recommendations you may wish to consider as you decide how you will personally react now and in the future to assessments and accountability systems. Keep in mind that as an individual instructional leader, you probably cannot change what has been and what is going to come as far as assessments and accountability systems are concerned. What you can do, however, is to come to grips with what you believe is right for students. Share that belief with others and, to the best of your ability, use that belief to guide your work.

Remember that what you can help change is the teaching. With all the talk about hiring and retaining quality teachers, there has been little attention given to how to improve the teaching. It is the teaching that will make a difference for the students, no matter how many tough education policies are passed. Your work as an instructional leader sits right on the edge of that reality.

LEADING IN A TIME OF TRANSITION

John Cage was an American composer, philosopher, poet, music theorist, artist, printmaker, amateur mycologist (study of fungi), and mushroom collector. He once said, "I can't understand why people are frightened of new ideas. I'm frightened of the old ones." In his spare time, Cage helped develop modern dance. He is most noted for his willingness to depart from the status quo. Never intimidated by new ideas, Cage could lead in a time of transition.

Did the new millennium usher in a time of transition in education with all the talk about 21st-century skills and student-centered learning? Perhaps. But, we are well into the new millennium and things in schools look pretty much the same as they did in the latter half of the 20th century. It is even difficult to find any statewide assessments that address 21st-century skills. The point here is that as an instructional leader you have to decide how you wish to lead in a time of transition. What you may well be thinking is: Transition from what?

- Transition from the watered-down education many students are receiving in the name of standards-based education to learning that is challenging, exciting, and meaningful.
- Transition from an imposed assessment system that uses flawed standardized tests and unreliable test scores to an assessment system based on student performance using a variety of measures to monitor individual progress over time.
- Transition from the top-down corporate model for profit to a child- and student-centered developmentally appropriate education model for learning.

THE NEED FOR COURAGE

Many educators work within the framework of what is expected. It is safe and it is what people are used to doing. Unfortunately, this is not where needed change in education will come from. A new conception of teaching and learning cannot be developed within this framework. The teaching gap will persist. The bridge to improving teaching methods will crack.

Throughout your career, there will be times when only you will know what you are thinking. You can keep those thoughts to yourself and no one will ever know the difference. But a decision to speak up for what is right for students is akin to transformation and what really matters in education. In the words of the Cowardly Lion: What makes an instructional leader stick his neck out? *Courage!* What makes an instructional leader innovate? *Courage!* What makes an instructional leader inspire needed change? *Courage!* What makes an instructional leader reignite the joy of teaching and learning? *Courage!* There is no wizard behind the curtain and no yellow brick road to guide you home safely. But, there are opportunities to stand up for what you believe is right for students. Those opportunities can be found in the work you do every day with students, teachers, parents, and other school leaders.

Picture This

You are at a meeting with administrators and other instructional leaders and the agenda is focused on whether there is a need to expand the school's test-prep curriculum. Changes at the state level have resulted in lower percentages of students who meet or exceed the new standards. The Board of Education and the superintendent have stated publicly that they are committed to making improvements. Most of the talk around the table is about the need to change overall curricula to better match state standards. So far, you have remained silent. What are you going to say?

From the standpoint of an instructional leader, you should say that you cannot go along with the need to narrow the curriculum, and here are my reasons why:

- Increasing the amount of time students spend preparing for state exams is not the answer. More time spent on test prep means less time teachers (and students) will have for meaningful, student-centered learning.

- We need to better understand where our students are having difficulty and to use that understanding to create better learning opportunities. The challenge is diagnostic, not systematic.
- It is wrong to exclude the teachers from this conversation because a decision made without their involvement and input disregards teachers as professionals. Would hospital administrators change surgical practice without involving the doctors?

Jay's voice reflects the thinking of all five instructional leaders with respect to helping yourself develop as an instructional leader.

"What you learn being an instructional leader day-to-day is your most valuable source of personal growth and leadership development. When you combine experiential learning with other forms of professional inquiry and self-reflection, you are on your way to helping yourself become a better instructional leader." ~ Jay

In-Your-Head-Quiz #7
(answer found on page 221)

Which of the four ways listed below has been emphasized throughout this book as being the best way for an instructional leader to develop on the job?

1. Networking with other instructional leaders.

2. Learning in the classroom.

3. Reading more research on teaching and learning.

4. Participating in the same professional development as the teachers.

JOURNAL REFLECTION

Before moving on to Chapter 7, take time to write in your journal. Here are some suggestions for possible topics and subtopics to write about. Select the one that you believe will give you the most insights at this point in your work and this stage of development as an instructional leader.

Knowing Yourself

If you read the article titled "Managing Oneself" (Drucker, 1999), take some time to write about what you learned about yourself.

- Be sure to include your strengths, how you work, your values, where you belong, and what you can contribute.

Communicating

Return to the section on Communicating. Review the part where you selected the five statements that describe you at your best as a communicator.

- Why did you pick those particular statements?
- What is one thing you need to do right away that you believe will help you communicate better?

Persuading and Inspiring

Write about a time when you persuaded an individual or a group to do something that you believe was good for students.

- What did you do that made a difference?

Do you inspire teachers?

- Why or why not?
- If you said, "sometimes," when are those times?

Giving and Receiving Feedback

Think of the last time you gave someone constructive feedback.

- How did it go?
- What did you learn from the experience?

Think of the last time you got some feedback about yourself that made you cringe a little.

- What was the nature of the feedback?
- Do you think it was valid?
- How can you use this feedback to improve?

Reacting to Assessments and the Accountability System

This section of Chapter 6 was designed to rile you up a bit. Why? Because it is time educators spoke up for education and what is right for students.

- Are you presently actively involved in any live or web-based discussion group that speaks out for child- and student-centered education?
  - How do you feel about expressing yourself this way?
- In your present job, have you ever took a stand (does not have to be something overwhelming) against one-size-fits-all testing? What happened?

TRY THIS: WHAT IS YOUR TRUE NORTH?

In Chapter 6, you are reminded of how important it is to develop yourself as an instructional leader.

Decide the kind of instructional leader you want to be and be that person all the time. Have a passion for what you believe is best for teaching and learning and stick with it.

Don't search for the right program or the best practice—search for a way to improve your work as an instructional leader.

To find your true north, try THIS:

- You will need a compass to steer you toward your own development.
- List five areas of instructional leadership that would help you improve. Hint: choose from the eight fundamental tenets that are essential for growth as an instructional leader that begin on page xiv.
- Label each improvement area that you selected a-b-c-d-e.
- Compare each improvement area to each other and circle the highest priority in each of the two match-ups. [a / b, a / c, a / d, a / e] [b / c, b / d, b / e] [c / d, c / e] [d / e]

- Count the highest priority for each improvement area.
- What is your true north?

What should be your first step in making this improvement area a priority?

 LEADERSHIP TEAM ACTIVITY

Let That Be a Lesson!

Purpose

Start with the end in mind.

- Instructional leaders will help each other improve in their ability to determine whether a lesson is effective or not, and to be able to explain why.
- Visualize the action needed to transfer seminar learning and understanding to current instructional leadership practice.

Perspective

- Just as teachers are isolated, so are instructional leaders. Rarely do instructional leaders ever watch the same lesson together and get a chance to discuss it for the purpose of improving their own observational skills, analysis, and descriptive feedback to teachers to improve instruction.

Challenge

- To be effective, an instructional leader must be able to distinguish between effective and noneffective teaching. Ironically, it has been proven repeatedly that when a number of educators all watch the same lesson episode, they often see it quite differently.

Plan

The basic steps for facilitating this single-focus seminar:

1. Provide time for a 60-minute seminar session with the leadership team and a follow-up session a week later.

(Continued)

(Continued)

2. Select an appropriate digital lesson episode (not a teacher from the school or district) for the leadership team to view together.
   a. The lesson episode should be about 10–15 minutes.
   b. The episode should be a basic lesson (one that is very typical of the teaching done in the school).
   c. Provide a little background about the lesson.
3. Establish the focus question to guide the viewing: Is this an example of an effective lesson? Why or why not?
4. After the viewing, conduct a simple yes/no survey as to whether or not it was an effective lesson.
5. Group the "Yes's" & the "No's" together.
6. Give them time to prepare their case as to why the lesson was or was not effective.
7. Give both groups time to present their case.

Personal and Team Connections

- Participants will be asked to connect their unique leadership challenges to the content of the seminar.
- The team will ask two essential questions: (1) What have we been learning? (2) How can we use this learning to strengthen our work as instructional leaders?

BRIDGE TO CHAPTER 7

What you do to help yourself improve as an instructional leader can increase your sense of satisfaction about your work. You need to be aware of signs of progress. This includes your communication decisions and your willingness to truly connect with the teachers and staff around you. Can you think of instances when you know for sure that your involvement with a teacher or group of teachers has inspired them to improve their teaching methods? When was the last time that you sought feedback about your performance as an instructional leader? Are you satisfied with the feedback you are giving teachers about their teaching?

School improvement plans often mention something about teachers working together as part of professional learning communities. Although the term "professional learning community" has come to mean different things to different people, there is one conclusion that is worthy of consideration. "The rise or fall of the professional learning community concept depends not on the merits of the concept itself, but on the most important element in the improvement of any school—the commitment and persistence of the educators within it" (DuFour, 2004, p. 11).

Chapter 7 is written especially for assistant superintendents of instruction, principals, assistant principals, and other administrators who are working with teachers to develop the commitment and persistence needed to support and sustain effective shared instructional leadership. Simply put, it means helping teachers to function as instructional leaders working with colleagues and administrators to improve teaching, affect student learning, and contribute to overall school improvement.

To be sure, there are recognizable conditions that must exist for shared instructional leadership to flourish and become part of a school's improvement process. Failure to address these conditions can greatly impact the ability of teachers to participate as instructional leaders. These conditions mirror the concepts normally associated with effective teamwork, which include recognizing the contributions of individuals, establishing relational trust, providing support for teams, upholding a commitment to a course of action, expecting consistent practice, seeking continuous improvement, and at the highest level, sustaining a culture of teaching that encourages collaboration with reflection and inquiry that goes beyond working collegially. The purpose of this chapter is to allow teachers to act in instructional leadership capacities to improve the methods needed to integrate better learning opportunities for students. That is what it will take to bridge the teaching gap.

CHAPTER SEVEN

Shared Instructional Leadership

"Instead of looking to the principal alone for instructional leadership, we need to develop leadership capacity among all members of the school community."

—Lambert, 2002 (p. 37)

INTRODUCTION

Implicit in the concept of shared instructional leadership used throughout this chapter is the belief that multiple leaders (teachers and administrators) must be involved in the development and continuance of a school's teaching and learning process. This implies a model of shared instructional leadership where leadership and leader are not the same. Shared instructional leadership is the opposite of one person, for example, the principal or the assistant superintendent of instruction, leading all facets of instructional improvement. This chapter will demonstrate why shared instructional leadership is at the cornerstone of bridging the teaching gap. You will be introduced to new ideas for strengthening the ability of teachers and administrators to work together to improve teaching and learning. The avenue for this extended learning is through the collaboration process needed to implement a school improvement plan.

Shared instructional leadership can be observed in action when teachers and administrators come together to address the needs of students, to analyze and evaluate an instructional problem, to develop a plan to improve instruction, to change methods where students are not succeeding, to learn about teaching in the classroom, to implement desired instructional change, or to make decisions that impact teaching and learning. If a school's culture of teaching includes shared instructional leadership, and that is not a given, you will most often find it in action in the work of either a committee or a team.

Interestingly enough, the term *committee* has come to mean a group of educators, teachers, and administrators that meet on a regular basis to address noninstructional matters such as school safety, student discipline, hiring staff, grading, scheduling, building concerns, and budgeting. Often these groups are referred to as standing committees. The use of the term *team*, however, has increased in leaps and bounds in recent years and implies a more collaborative process. These days, a team is more than just a group of teachers advising the administration. With respect to the development of lasting school improvement, the distinction between the work of a committee and teamwork has evolved beyond mere semantics.

As you begin to rethink the concept of shared instructional leadership, think of where shared instructional leadership is located in your school or district. To help you do this, you are asked to complete the grid found below. Some of the most common examples of shared instructional leadership have been placed in the grid, but you are encouraged to add others that are directly related to improving teaching and learning. Time spent describing the purpose of each group and checking how the group is led will open your eyes to the full spectrum of shared instructional leadership in your school or district.

Shared Instructional Leadership Example: Lesson Design Team	*Purpose* Framework for planning lessons	*Led by (check only one)* Admin. / Teacher / Both*
1. Grade-Level Team		
2. Department Team		
3. Curriculum Team		
4. Research/Study Team		
5. Lesson Study Team		
6. School Improvement Team		
7.		
8.		
9.		
10.		

HOW SCHOOL LEADERS AFFECT STUDENT LEARNING

 "The central job, and also the most difficult, for school leaders is to shape the school's culture to focus unremitting attention on student learning. Thus, in 2004, we set out to find out how school leaders affect student learning.

We talked with over a thousand district office staff, school administrators, teachers, parents, and other stakeholders across the country, and we surveyed more than 8,000 principals and teachers in 164 schools, all within a random sample of nine states that included nearly every type of district.

We found that changing a school's culture requires *shared or distributed leadership,* which engages many stakeholders in major improvement roles, and *instructional leadership,* in which administrators take responsibility for shaping improvements at the classroom level." (Seashore Lewis & Wahlstrom, 2011, p. 52)

---

*If you check both, it means that an administrator and a teacher are co-leaders or an administrator and a teacher take turns leading the group. The terms facilitator or chair may apply.

You are probably not surprised by the number of instruction-ally related teams/committees that exist in your school or district. Shared instructional leadership, mostly through the work of teams, has developed exponentially in response to factors such as the need and demand for more teacher involvement in the decision-making process, the push for greater collaboration, the need for extended leadership to carry out school improvement plans, and the internal and external pressures to increase test scores. Although unilateral decision-making, at least on the surface, has gone the way of ditto machines and 16mm film projectors, not all teachers and administrators believe shared instructional leader-ship is a done deal.

The grid column that is most revealing about the state of shared instructional leadership in schools these days is the third column—the one that deals with who is leading the group. What does the bal-ance of leadership look like? If most of the shared instructional leadership groups are led by administrators, there is probably rea-son to believe that the leadership approach is still functioning more like an advisory group. Although this type of leadership approach may be effective for making some decisions, for example, deciding the format for report cards, it will not result in teachers taking more responsibility for improving teaching methods. It must be said that only instructional leadership that is truly shared between teachers and administrators has the potential to help close the teaching gap. Without this level of commitment, most plans to improve teaching and learning will remain just plans.

EDUCATIONAL IMPROVEMENT THROUGH TEACHER LEADERSHIP

"Teacher leadership is the process by which teachers, indi-vidually or collectively, influence their colleagues, princi-pals, and other members of the school communities to improve teaching and learning practices with the aim of increased student learning and achievement.

Recognition of teacher leadership comes from new under-standings about organizational development and leadership that suggest active involvement of individuals at all levels and within all domains of an organization is necessary if change is to take hold.

Educational improvement at the level of instruction necessarily involves leadership by teachers in classrooms and with peers. In addition, teacher leadership has expanded to include roles ranging from assisting with the management of schools to evaluating educational initiatives and facilitating professional learning communities." ~ York-Barr and Duke (2004, p. 300)

STRENGTHENING SHARED INSTRUCTIONAL LEADERSHIP

#8: A Shortsighted Vision (National Comprehensive Center for Teacher Quality, 2007)

Betsy Henry is an experienced science teacher in a low-performing high school in a midsized Southern town. During the course of her career, she has taught all grade levels and most science classes in the high school. For the last few years, she has been teaching ninth grade, which is the entry point into the high school. She has some concerns about the ninth-grade program and does not think it effectively meets the needs of the students. Betsy would like to make it more learner-centered and to encourage the ninth-grade teachers to include more hands-on, active, real-world instructional strategies that would engage their students.

Betsy's high school is in the Coffee County school district. Many of the families in the area work in low-skilled jobs in nearby tobacco-processing plants. The Coffee County school district administration wants to better prepare students for future educational and employment opportunities and is trying to improve student learning through a districtwide focus on instructional leadership. The superintendent introduced Betsy's principal to the concept of teacher leadership and asked him to identify a group of qualified teachers in his school to serve as leaders for improving instruction in an effort to improve student achievement.

The principal then appointed Betsy as lead teacher of the ninth-grade academic team. Within her new position, she would have release time to work with teachers and a small stipend for additional duties. Betsy had no desire either for a title or for serving in an administrative capacity; however, she accepted because she viewed this new position as a way to implement her vision for a learner-centered instructional program across disciplines that would benefit ninth-grade students.

Unfortunately, not all went as planned. As soon as Betsy began to make changes, she encountered the following obstacles:

Colleagues. Her colleagues were not willing to work with her on the learner-centered project. They resented her new title and position as well as the benefits that came with her new responsibilities. In addition, they did not want to make changes and said they would just do what was required by the principal. They excluded her from team camaraderie, and she felt isolated from the collegiality she had enjoyed when she was an equal member of the team.

Principal. The principal was not available for support. It seemed impossible to schedule a time with him to discuss plans and to report progress, and he was not willing to secure the resources she needed for staff training. When Betsy created a new block schedule for ninth graders, which was more appropriate for the new hands-on teaching strategies, she encountered a glitch, and the principal showed his displeasure by taking the scheduling responsibility away from her.

Time and place. Betsy was always pressed for time, even though she was released from a weekly study-hall duty. She was afraid that her own teaching was suffering because of the time she was spending on implementing the new program. In addition, she had trouble scheduling a common time for the ninth-grade team to meet since everyone had a different planning period. Further, the members of the ninth-grade team were scattered all over the school in their subject department wings, so it was hard for her to have informal discussions in passing or to visit classrooms to observe and give feedback on instructional practices.

Betsy is frustrated but determined to make her idea for learner-centered teaching work! Her principal also wants to improve instruction in his school. How can Betsy and her principal learn together? What skills does Betsy need to lead instructional improvement? How can Betsy's principal support her as she strives to be an effective teacher leader? These and other questions pertaining to strengthening instructional leadership will be answered throughout the remained of this chapter.

Strengthening Shared Instructional Leadership With Grade and Department Chairs

To provide a frame of reference for strengthening shared instructional leadership, think of the best teacher leader you know. This could be a natural leader, that is, someone who the teachers go to but does not have a formal leadership position, or a teacher assigned a leadership position such as a grade or department chair. On the lines below, list three reasons why you think this person is the best teacher leader you know.

1. _____

2. _____

3. _____

Think about your three reasons. These reasons are important for you to understand because they represent your concept of an effective teacher leader. The development of shared instructional leadership is influenced greatly by the perceptions of the school leaders. For example, if you listed: "respected by peers," "can establish positive working relationships," or "good problem solver," you value human relations skills. The teacher leader has good people skills. If, conversely, you listed: "content expert," "curricular knowledge," or "master teacher," you value educational skills.

"Teachers can be empowered to become instructional leaders by demonstrating those thoughts in actions and conversations. For example, saying things like: "thanks for taking a leadership role at a staff meeting"; "we need instructional leaders like you"; and "one of the challenges of being an instructional leader is overcoming complacency." ~ Bill

GRADE AND DEPARTMENT LEVEL

Shared instructional leadership, if it truly exists in a school or district, can usually be found at the grade or department level. The two most common examples of teacher leadership are grade and department chairs. For this reason, the positions of grade and department chairs will provide the context for a focused inquiry into how to strengthen shared instructional leadership. Keep in mind that some or all of the conditions for improving shared instructional leadership with grade and department chairs also apply to other teacher leaders such as team leaders, lead teachers, teachers on special assignment, and other instructional specialists.

Traditionally, the role of a grade or department chair has been more about representation than leadership, where the teacher leaders were expected to manage the grade level or department. The job descriptions of grade and department chairs, if they existed at all, were mainly focused on noninstructional matters. Below is an example of a more recent job description for grade and department chairs.

1. Disseminates information received from building administration.

2. Provides leadership in the development and implementation of curriculum.

3. Works with the administration to develop priorities for academic improvement.

4. Assists in staff development activities.

5. Provides leadership in the analysis of data and the development of strategies for academic achievement.

6. Assists in the development of the master schedule.

7. Acts as a liaison between the administration and the staff to ensure effective communication.

8. Assists the administration in ordering supplies and equipment.

9. Maintains inventory of supplies and equipment.

10. Attends all meetings called by the administration.

11. Coordinates and schedules meetings, agenda, and provides a summary of meetings to administration.

12. Assists in the selection of personnel for the building, as requested.

As you can see, this list of job responsibilities does include some attention to instructional matters, for example, development and implementation of curriculum, but most of the prescribed duties are still devoted to making sure there is a strong link between the administration and teachers. Although the liaison approach to teacher leadership has merit for maintaining continuity and stability in a school, this relationship is not sufficient to develop the level of shared instructional leadership needed to actualize the direction established in a school improvement plan or to connect grade-level, department, building, and district goals.

Today grade and department chairs are being asked to shift to a leadership role in which they continue to effectively manage the grade level or department but that management becomes secondary to the role of being an instructional leader. The major elements of grade and department chair instructional leadership include developing a shared vision; using data to improve student learning and promote professional development, align standards, curriculum, instruction, and assessment; and promoting continuous and sustainable improvement (Kelley, 2010, p. 25). That is a tall order with often a short plan for accomplishing it.

Here is the problem. Because of the urgency these days surrounding the school improvement process, many administrators are asking grade and department chairs to get more involved in sharing the leadership needed to accomplish building and district goals. This is especially true when it comes to following through with improvement initiatives in the classroom. Asking grade and department chairs to assume more instructional leadership responsibilities often goes above and beyond their current job descriptions and levels of competencies. The conditions under which grade and department chairs can develop as instructional leaders are presented below with the understanding that they are essential for this type of role transformation to occur.

Grade and department chairs must first have a clear understanding of what they are expected to do as far as shared instructional leadership is concerned. These expectations must be written down in a revised job description that is clarified in conversations between administrators and grade and department chairs. It is possible that changes in the job description, even when done gradually, may cause some teacher leaders to decline the upgraded leadership position.

Second, principals must communicate any changes in the role of grade or department chairs to the entire faculty. It is essential that classroom teachers understand why their grade or department chairs are taking on some new responsibilities and the parameters of their authority. Grade and department chairs often confess that lack of authority makes it difficult for them to carry out certain responsibilities with their colleagues. For example, some grade and department chairs are asked to monitor lesson plans. Unless this expectation is fully understood, some teachers may balk at having to show their lesson plans to a grade or department chair. You can see how this could easily play out with other instructionally related matters where grade or department chairs lack a recognized line of authority.

Although it is vitally important for everyone (teachers and administrators) to understand the transition to greater shared instructional leadership, it is also essential that grade and department chairs receive ongoing opportunities to improve their instructional leadership skills. One of the best ways to approach this need is through the use of customized instructional leadership seminars with assistant superintendents of instruction, principals, assistant principals, and grade and department chairs all learning together. It sends a clear message to staff that school leaders are working together to improve instruction.

Possible areas of study might include articulating school goals, leading instructional change, building capacity for teamwork, using data wisely, conducting collaborative inquiry, and dealing with difficult people and resistance to desired instructional change. A valuable resource for helping grade and department chairs understand their role as an instructional leader was introduced back in Chapter 5, The 7 Disciplines for Strengthening Instruction (Wagner, 2004). These 7 Disciplines can form the basis for developing customized instructional leadership seminars.

In one school, the instructional leaders fine-tuned their theories of action using a protocol developed by the Harvard Change Leadership Group called Step Back Consulting. This procedure put instructional leaders in triads as they took turns sharing their instructional leadership plans and reacting to each other as consultants. The protocol is structured by time and role changes (from presenters to consultants) and even includes a way for listeners to take on the plan as if it were their own.

Feedback gleaned from this highly interactive experience is very helpful to instructional leaders determined to energize their action plans while in progress. Once again, the power of collaboration is not only used to help team members do their jobs better, but as a stimulus for professional learning. That is the point to keep in mind.

COLLABORATION TO BRIDGE THE TEACHING GAP

 "Improvements in teaching are most likely to occur where there are opportunities for teachers to work together and to learn from each other. Working with colleagues not only dispels feelings of professional isolation but assists in enhancing practice. Teachers are more able to implement new ideas within the context of supportive collaborative relationships or partnerships. Collaboration among teachers strengthens resolve, permits vulnerabilities, and carries people through the frustrations that accompany change in its early stages." ~ Hargreaves, 1994; Harris, 2002 (p. 102)

COLLABORATION

One of the leadership areas where most grade and department chairs welcome help is facilitating collaboration, that is, teamwork. We know much more about the conditions under which teachers develop to the benefit of themselves and students than we do about developing collaboration among teachers (Harris, 2002). It is not easy leading one's peers, and yet collaboration is an essential part of closing the learning and teaching gap because it improves the quality of student learning by improving the quality of teaching. Teachers working together are more apt to take the risks needed to improve teaching methods and to support each other trying new ideas in the classroom. So how do you help grade and department chairs, often with limited time with and access to the teachers in their group, learn how to foster collaboration?

Because teamwork does not happen naturally in most schools, the condition of learning most closely associated with helping someone learn how to foster collaboration with peers is modeling. Opportunities for collaborative learning should be a core activity for the expansion of leadership capacity. Grade and department chairs need to be a part of a group (e.g., leadership team or study group) where they can see collaboration in action. It is through this experience that grade and department chairs may learn firsthand about the various levels of collaboration from building relational trust to sustaining a culture of teamwork.

Collaboration in dialogue, behavior, and action can provide sources of feedback and comparison that prompt grade and department chairs to reflect on their own leadership practice. Learning about collaboration could begin when grade and department chairs observe the process as members of the school improvement team. This type of active learning might include observing how the principal shares important information, acknowledges the contributions of others, and admits that there may be times when the team knows more than she does. As participant observers, grade and department chairs learn from fellow team members who rely on each other for help and support, constructively explore their differences on certain issues, express their feelings freely, listen attentively to the opinions of others, and reflect openly as individuals and as a group.

Grade and department chairs who want to learn how to facilitate collaboration with colleagues often value access to protocols designed to empower all group members and promote a genuine feeling of working together. Two examples of protocols that are helpful to the tasks of collaborative planning and data-based decision making are the Tuning Protocol (McDonald, Mohr, Dichter, & McDonald, 2003) and the Collaborative Learning Cycle (Wellman & Lipton, 2004). Both of these protocols have a format structure that gives voice to even the most hesitant members of a team and will help the members of a group begin to function as a team. Both of these protocols, and there are many others available, are based on the concept of reflective inquiry. It is the reflection that separates true collaboration, that is, teamwork, from mere collegiality.

As the chairs gain experience facilitating collaboration with their teachers, they may ask another school leader to sit in on one of their grade or department meetings. Constructive feedback cannot only help them to improve their skills as a team leader, it is a low-risk way to learn more about the process of facilitating collaboration. In this same vein, a simple survey given to grade and department teachers can help the chairs discover whether the teachers are feeling like a team. It is also a good idea for grade and department chairs to talk to each other about collaboration. An ideal time for such a discussion would be after all of the chairs had facilitated a similar collaborative task, such as a goal-setting session held on a professional development day. Some principals generate these opportunities by suggesting to grade or department chairs that they use a particular method for strategic collaboration. Learning more about facilitating teamwork is enhanced through shared techniques and collaborative reflection.

Grade and department chairs must continually have access to the best information and research about teaching and learning. Classroom teachers depend on their teacher leaders to help them select effective teaching methods and to help them work together in order to change methods where students are not succeeding. Providing this information is not simply a matter of moving journal articles, research reports, and books into the hands of grade and department chairs. Teachers developing as instructional leaders need to be given opportunities to discuss teaching and learning in seminar-like conditions with colleagues and others who can stretch their thinking and understanding about teaching and learning.

Quite often, the greatest challenge facing grade and department chairs is working with teachers to make needed instructional changes. This point was brought home very clearly in Case Illustration #8: A Shortsighted Vision. Administrators, especially principals, must be in-tune with the struggles that grade or department chairs face when they attempt to lead colleagues into areas that require substantial change in beliefs and practice. Support and guidance during these times are essential to success, and it may require establishing a line of authority that will sanction grade or department chairs to follow through with teachers who are reluctant to cooperate or prefer to adopt an attitude of passive resistance. Grade and department chairs cannot be expected to facilitate change perceived by the teachers as second order solely on their own. Administrators should lead the way by talking with the faculty about the impending change and clarify the role that grade and department chairs will play in helping to implement that change.

WORKING RELATIONSHIPS

The final condition for strengthening shared instructional leadership involves the day-to-day working relationships between grade and department chairs and building level administrators. The goal is to build instructional leadership and problem-solving capacities. Principals and assistant principals who openly value the role and work of grade and department chairs empower them in their leadership tasks. This level of relational support and trust is enhanced when administrators promote and facilitate collaboration in their own leadership work with teachers and other school leaders. In other words, they are a working example of collaborative leadership. This behavior and attitude allows the focus of shared leadership to shift from micromanaging the details to one of supporting the larger goal—improving student learning. This style of leadership does not go unnoticed by the faculty and helps to affirm the role that shared instructional leadership plays in the overall success of school improvement initiatives.

This condition also includes providing ongoing support and guidance for grade and department chairs moving forward with their role as an instructional leader. The support could be something as simple as an informal conversation about how things are going to a more structured opportunity for individual coaching. Leading colleagues is tough work, especially when there is pressure to make improvements or implement a new approach. Grade and department chairs must feel that someone understands what they are going through and is willing to listen and help when the need arises.

As a group, it is a good idea for grade and department chairs to meet together with the principal or assistant principal at least once a month. The agenda needs to be flexible allowing for collective planning, the sharing of ideas, addressing problems of practice, and developing instructional leadership strategies. Depending on how these meetings are handled, they can build up or tear down the trust and respect that is required for a positive working relationship and effective shared instructional leadership.

"We can empower teachers to develop as instructional leaders when we give them opportunities to work in other classrooms and to interact with a variety of teaching professionals. They have a chance to learn how to work with a range of personalities and discover the importance of teacher collaboration." ~Anita

SHARED INSTRUCTIONAL LEADERSHIP IN ACTION

#9: Vision Becomes Reality

Joan McCabe is a teacher and fourth-grade chair in the K–6 Water Elementary School, located in a large rural/suburban school district. She and the other grade-level chairs in Grades 2–6 were asked by the principal to work with the teachers at their respective grade levels to develop formative assessments in reading and mathematics. The principal told Joan and the other grade-level chairs that the purpose of the formative assessments was twofold: (1) to better inform teaching and (2) to reduce the discrepancy between report card grades and results on state mandated tests. The work was to be done during a 10-day period over the summer, and all teachers who worked on the assessments would receive professional development credit and a stipend.

Joan and the other fourth-grade teachers worked hard over the summer to prepare classroom assessments that were aligned with the state standards in both reading and mathematics. The formative assessments they created also included many of the literacy and numeracy concepts and skills that the teachers knew from experience were difficult for children to grasp. Although some of the fourth-grade teachers expressed concerns about the amount of time it would take to give these formative assessments and analyze the results, the formative assessments were completed on time along with those from the other grade levels.

The principal collected all of the formative assessments by the end of the summer and thanked the teachers and grade-level chairs for a job well done. The principal even mentioned that this work was a fine example of the school's belief in shared instructional leadership. Joan was pleased with the work that the fourth-grade teachers had done and was prepared to help the teachers implement the formative assessments when the new term began in September.

At the first faculty meeting of the new school year, the principal announced that the formative assessments in reading and mathematics, developed over the summer, would be implemented the week of November 8, just before the first 10-week marking period. Joan was apprehensive about using the formative assessments and spent considerable amount of time working with the teachers on strategies for administering and analyzing the assessments. This effort paid off as both Joan and her fourth-grade teachers got through their first experience with grade-level assessments quite successfully. The teachers, although some were still grousing about how the added assessments compromise instructional time, felt that their teaching was impacted very positively by having this assessment information.

You may think this case illustration is unrealistic because everything went so smoothly, and ordinarily, you might be right. So let us peel back the layers of this onion to see why things worked out so well for Joan and the fourth-grade teachers. First, you need to understand that Joan and the other grade-level chairs were carefully selected by the teachers and the principal for these teacher leadership positions. Like Joan, the grade-level chairs possessed a deep understanding of how students learn and were recognized by their peers as having demonstrated leadership qualities. The grade-level chairs served for a period of 3 years and were members of the principal's leadership team, which met for 1 hour each month. Each team meeting was devoted to some aspect of instructional leadership, such as leading desired instructional change.

The principal in this case illustration did not leave the effectiveness of grade-level chairs to chance. She not only worked collectively with the grade-level chairs, she provided individual help and guidance in the form of coaching whenever there was a need for additional support. Grade-level chairs were not expected to be cracker-jack teacher leaders just because they were given the title and a new job description. The principal knew that ongoing professional leadership development tailored to the needs of the needs of the grade chairs was essential to the success and development of shared instructional leadership in the building.

Joan's ability to implement instructional change, in this case, the formative assessments, did not happen by accident. Prior to becoming a grade-level chair, Joan had been given an opportunity to lead teachers serving as the co-chair of the school's standing committee on literacy. There were a number of times during that experience that Joan and her co-chair had to deal with some resistance to change. Her colleagues all agreed that Joan had done a nice job leading the group.

Lastly, the classroom teachers at each grade level were brought into the shared instructional leadership development process through frequent opportunities to discuss collaboration and teamwork at both grade-level meetings and whole-school faculty meetings. Improving teamwork meant working with the team members as well as the team leaders. For instance, one of the reasons that things went so smoothly in this case illustration is because the teachers were given an opportunity to work out the kinks together. The teachers in the Water Elementary School did not need to have an administrator standing over them; they were able to take responsibility for improving teaching and learning. This case illustrates what Roland Barth (2001) meant when he said, "When teachers lead, principals extend their own capacity" (p. 443).

ALIGNED INSTRUCTIONAL LEADERSHIP TEAM FOR SCHOOL IMPROVEMENT

Much has been written about school improvement, but little consideration has been given to the collaborative delivery of instructional leadership needed to make this process work for students and teachers. In a culture of teaching, which often is characterized by isolation and professional autonomy, the teamwork and cooperative effort needed to achieve a common goal, such as increasing the number of mastery level students, or to implement a new teaching initiative, such as extending and refining thinking skills, is a challenge for even the best education leaders.

A natural extension of shared instructional leadership is the formation of a school-based instructional leadership team for school improvement. Members of the team should include the principal (often the point person), assistant principal, grade and department chairs, learning specialists, and other instructional coaches or leaders in the building. The team would typically meet three to four times per month, with its main responsibility to guide the school improvement process.

Fenton (2011) underlines the need for a school-based instructional leadership team when he writes, "Principals cannot lead schools to make breakthrough achievement gains on their own: the support of an aligned instructional leadership team is crucial" (para. 1). An instructional leadership team is aligned when the members of the team share the same vision, such as student-centered learning; constantly reinforce the same messages to teachers and staff; model the norms and behaviors consistent with true collaboration, such as relational trust and ongoing support; maintain effective lines of communication; and are genuinely reflective in their work as individuals and team members. In other words, they have their act together.

Using a shared decision-making model, the aligned instructional leadership team provides a support structure for transforming school improvement goals systematically into action that will improve learning and teaching. The team does not do this in a vacuum as all teachers, staff, and parents have a right to know about the details of this critical improvement process. The team, however, does function as an internal accountability system with all members dedicated to achieving the school improvement goals and making the plan work for students and teachers.

In order to guide the school improvement process, the focus of an aligned instructional leadership team needs to be on three domains in particular:

1. Developing the school improvement plan;

2. Clarifying the school improvement goals and initiatives; and

3. Providing stability and support throughout the improvement process.

As traditional leadership practice sometimes exhibits an inability to operationalize these domains, the rest of this section is devoted to a discussion of each of them individually. Within each domain, one or two problems of practice will be explored with some suggestions for solving them.

The first domain of an aligned instructional leadership team is developing the school improvement plan. Collaboration is the basis for bringing together all members of the team to contribute to the development of the plan. Besides making sure that school goals are aligned with district goals and written with language that is clear and specific, it is very important for the entire team to carefully consider and describe all of the initiatives (sometimes called action plans) that will need to be implemented. Because the school improvement process is cyclical in nature, some of the goals and initiatives are new and some are ongoing.

The development of the initiatives (new and sustained) is very important, and if done in isolation, can create real problems in the following year. Each initiative recommended for inclusion into the school improvement plan needs to be carefully scrutinized to make sure that it is the best way to support a particular goal and that it is doable in terms of time, resources, and know-how. This part of the development process cannot be rushed, and even when done thoroughly, it may result in some differences of opinion about the best way to make improvements. This is the time to work out the differences, philosophical or otherwise, and not after the plan has been approved by the board of education. Teachers are often justified in saying that there are just too many instructional initiatives in the building and many are not well coordinated.

Before the final decision is made about the initiatives to be included in a school improvement plan, put all of the goals and support initiatives on the wall so team members can view them in their entirety. Once again, the first consideration should always be whether the initiatives are appropriate for the goals. Are these initiatives the best for students? Next, it is important to look at the initiatives from the point of view of the teachers who will have to implement them. Are the initiatives doable? Will the teachers have the time, resources, and support to address each initiative properly? Finally, instructional leaders need to ask themselves if they can effectively coordinate all of the initiatives (new and sustained) and how the initiatives fit with programs that are already in place.

The second domain of an aligned instructional leadership team is clarifying the school improvement goals and initiatives. Every teacher, staff member, and parent needs to understand what is in the school improvement plan for the upcoming year. The first step is to make sure there is a clear vision of what is trying to be accomplished. Why were the goals selected in the first place and how will the support initiatives make a difference for students? Some schools post their school improvement goals in the entrance to the building along with quarterly progress reports. Everyone connected with the school knows where and how improvements are sought and the progress made.

When teachers clarify the school improvement plan, they are most interested in specifics about the initiatives. How is this plan going to impact my work as a teacher? So, for example, if one of the initiatives is for the teachers to attend a professional development program aimed at improving reading comprehension, the teachers will want details about the program such as the frequency of the sessions and the nature of the professional learning. To be sure, any significant change in the way reading is taught will create some tension between the teachers. Ideally, teacher questions would have been addressed by instructional leaders prior to the completion of the school improvement plan.

Teachers will also be concerned when they feel overwhelmed by the extent of the initiatives. This you can bank on. Most of the tension is generated when teachers feel there are too many new initiatives piled on the initiatives sustained from the previous year(s). As mentioned before, this is why all members of the instructional leadership team need to take a close look at the big picture when it comes to school improvement. Uncoordinated initiatives or too many initiatives can seriously undermine efforts to make continuous improvements. Even the most dedicated teachers will get uptight when they feel that their time is hijacked or they are frequently pulled out of class for meetings or workshops.

The third domain of an aligned instructional leadership team is providing stability and support throughout the improvement process. Greater stability means clearer expectations that are reinforced with more opportunities to address misconceptions and if need be, offer additional support structures and procedures. So, now the school year is underway and the teachers are busy implementing the new improvement initiatives, sustaining the old ones, and teaching all of their classes. If the demands associated with the improvement initiatives are reasonable, things should go smoothly. However, when the sense of urgency rises in the building, so do the anxiety levels of many of the teachers.

Like any organization, a school must operate with a reasonable amount of stability so staff can carry out their work effectively. Pressures caused by time constraints, personnel conflicts, scheduling problems, lack of resources, too many meetings and workshops, and other factors related to the improvement process may affect the equilibrium of a school. Teachers may react negatively to these pressures expressing frustration and dissatisfaction with their work. Members of an aligned instructional leadership team must be able to read the pressure gauge, so to speak, in an effort to prevent or diffuse these feelings of frustration.

Working alongside teachers, instructional leaders must not only be concerned with the educational problems that may arise, but the people problems that might be developing. An instructional leadership team is aligned when there is true collaboration and that means building relational trust and providing ongoing support to meet individual and group needs. Team members remind each other about how important it is to take the pulse of the teachers and to respond quickly when they see it going up. Often the leadership response is just to provide an opportunity for teachers to talk about their work and to encourage them to bring out any problems or issues that may be frustrating them. It sounds like asking for trouble, but it is really asking how to keep out of trouble.

Just to be clear, sensitivity to the pressures teachers may be feeling about continuous school improvement does not mean backing off on an important initiative at the first sign of trouble. Nor does it mean ignoring the teachers' feelings. One of the benefits of having an aligned instructional leadership team is the ability to talk with other instructional leaders about making these kinds of decisions. To be successful, instructional leaders will need to help each other expand the use of strategies that integrate teacher development and school improvement.

Listen to one principal describe his belief about leading the school improvement process: "School improvement is not an event. It is an ongoing process that has no end. As a principal, parents, and community members would repeatedly ask me, 'When can we stop our comprehensive school-wide literacy initiative?' I would answer, 'We will stop emphasizing reading, writing, thinking and speaking when our parents repeatedly complain that their children are reading too fast with comprehension that is too high and when our students' writing skills are so superior that they are regularly winning Pulitzers and other literary awards.' Smiles would erupt throughout the audience. They got it. They understood that literacy skills can always be improved and so can our schools" (Riddile, 2010, The Bottom Line section, para. 1).

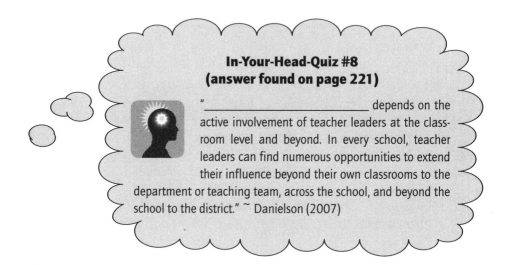

**In-Your-Head-Quiz #8
(answer found on page 221)**

"_____ depends on the active involvement of teacher leaders at the classroom level and beyond. In every school, teacher leaders can find numerous opportunities to extend their influence beyond their own classrooms to the department or teaching team, across the school, and beyond the school to the district." ~ Danielson (2007)

JOURNAL REFLECTION

Before moving on to Chapter 8, take time to write in your journal. Here are some suggestions for possible topics and subtopics to write about. Select the one that you believe will give you the most insights at this point in your work.

Shared Instructional Leadership

Think about where instructional leadership is shared in your school. You may wish to look back at the grid you completed on page 155.

- Think of some aspect of your school where you would like to see more shared instructional leadership. Explain why you feel this way and what you could do to move in that direction.

Grade and Department Chairs

Think about how grade or department chairs in your school are developed.

- Who are the most effective instructional leaders?
- What do they do that helps set them apart as far as instructional leadership is concerned?

Instructional Leadership Team

- If your school has an instructional leadership team, describe how it functions. Be sure to include one way that the effectiveness of the team could be better aligned with school improvement goals and one way that the team effectiveness could be strengthened.
- If your school does not have an instructional leadership team, do you think that one needs to be organized? What could you do to help make that happen?

Collaboration

- In your school, are there opportunities for teachers to collaborate, discuss, and network? Explain.
- Is there time set aside for teachers to reflect on their practice with colleagues? Explain.

TRY THIS: REALITY CHECK

When you think about Chapter 7, you might be thinking, "Yes, I am always willing to share instructional leadership, especially with teachers."

Keep in mind, you are talking about a model of shared instructional leadership where leadership and leader are not the same.

How is it that in many schools the teachers do not feel a sense of genuine shared instructional leadership. Is it possible to strengthen shared instructional leadership without knowing how the teachers really feel?

If you are serious about sharing instructional leadership, you might want to try THIS:

- Make a list of the last three instructional improvement initiatives that you were involved in as a leader.

(Continued)

(Continued)

- Next to each initiative, write down how you shared the instructional leadership from the beginning to the end.
- With your list in hand, ask some of the teachers and staff members involved about shared instructional leadership.
    - Did they feel they were a part of the decision-making process?
    - Were their ideas and suggestions sought and considered before a final decision was made?
- Compare the two lists.

Next time you start an improvement initiative, put shared instructional leadership on the front burner.

 LEADERSHIP TEAM ACTIVITY

We Are What We Say We Are

Purpose

Start with the end in mind.

- The instructional leadership team or school improvement team is working as a true team with a high level of shared instructional leadership.
- Visualize the action needed to transfer seminar learning and understanding to current instructional leadership practice.

Perspective

- The true litmus test for shared instructional leadership is how members of a district or school leadership team believe they match up to the three domains of an aligned instructional leadership team with respect to school improvement. The goal is to ensure that "we are what we say we are."

Challenge

- To be effective, an instructional leader must be able to demonstrate the willingness and ability to collaborate with other members of the district or school's instructional leadership or school improvement team.

Plan

The basic steps for facilitating this single-focus seminar:

1. Provide time for a 60-minute seminar session with the leadership team.

2. Prior to the seminar, distribute a copy of the discussion of the three domains of an aligned instructional leadership team found on pages 170–174 in the book. Ask the leaders to assess each domain as they see the instructional leadership or school improvement team in action.

3. Working in small groups, compare assessments. Where do we agree? Disagree?

4. Each group is asked to report out areas of alignment and areas that seem to be out of alignment.

5. Post the alignments and the nonalignments.

6. Facilitate a collaborative reflection about what could be done to increase shared instructional leadership. What is the role of the leadership team?

Personal and Team Connections

- Participants will be asked to connect their unique leadership challenges to the content of the seminar.
- The team will ask two essential questions: (1) What have we been learning? (2) How can we use this learning to strengthen our work as instructional leaders?

BRIDGE TO CHAPTER 8

The importance of shared instructional leadership cannot be overstated. The combined efforts of all instructional leaders in a school are needed to improve teaching methods and create better learning opportunities for students—the path to closing the teaching gap. This is why each school must have a system in place that allows instructional leaders to meet together on a regular basis and an in-house structure that supports the conditions for improving instructional leadership and instructional leaders. All instructional leaders, teachers and administrators, must learn as much as possible about leading teams and facilitating collaboration. These two leadership practices cannot be left to chance; they are the means to an end—increased student learning and greater success as a teacher.

School improvement is not only the process for accomplishing important goals tied to teaching and learning; it is, by its very nature, a plan of intended action whereby educators can learn how to work as a team across all grade levels and departments. Working on the school improvement plan should be thought of as a training ground for learning about collaboration and reflective inquiry. The goals we seek in public education depend on collaboration, not isolation. As asserted by Blasé and Blasé (2004), "Today's most successful schools are fast becoming centers of shared inquiry and decision making; teachers are moving toward a collective—not an individual—practice of teaching" (p. 3).

The purpose of Chapter 8 is to bring even greater meaning to the concept of instructional leadership. To do this, you will first travel "back to the future" through a series of instructional leadership success stories (scenarios) taken from coaching experience. Each story deals with some aspect of instructional leadership development presented in this book. You will be able to follow the path of a number of instructional leaders as they responded to challenges related to school improvement. The emphasis is on how they used specific instructional leadership practices to achieve success. Ideally, these accounts will be a source of inspiration as you think about what the future holds for you as a developing instructional leader.

The final section of this chapter will tighten the connection between becoming a better instructional leader and closing the teaching gap. It begins with an analysis of the success stories guided by answers to the question: When is good instructional leadership going on? A follow-up inspection of your own instructional leadership practices may help you to recognize and leverage your strengths as you continue to develop as an instructional leader.

CHAPTER EIGHT

Closing the Teaching Gap

"We are inspired by the insights and courage of those working to change the culture of teaching, but we are sobered by the obstacles they face."

—Stigler and Hiebert, 2009 (p. 181)

LEARNING FROM SUCCESS STORIES

This book has been about a core of instructional leadership practices recognized as exemplary. The practices form a common ground of instructional leadership and have been taken from a wide range of experience, research, and coaching. Putting these practices into action cannot only help you become a better instructional leader, they can help you improve the methods used by teachers. The premise from the outset of the book is that if you can help improve the methods used by teachers, you will, in fact, be helping to close the teaching gap and increase student learning in ways that will satisfy learners, teachers, administrators, and the public.

Core Instructional Leadership Practices Recognized as Exemplary

Increase your understanding of learning	Ensure a widely shared vision of learning	Get into classrooms as much as possible
Help teachers learn more about teaching	Increase your understanding of the culture of teaching	Increase your understanding of change leadership
Work with teachers to change methods where students are not succeeding	Work with teachers to create better learning opportunities for students	Strengthen shared instructional leadership
Use data to improve teaching	Develop a theory of action	Be a reflective practitioner

Coaching instructional leaders has provided a rare opportunity to study core instructional leadership practices in-depth over a period of time. These experiences have been consolidated into a series of Success Stories taken from Coaching. Each scenario starts with an instructional leadership challenge that surfaced during a coaching relationship and recounts how instructional leaders responded to similar instructional challenges in order to close the teaching gap. Although the instructional leaders in these stories are fictional, the scenarios are authentic, representing composites of real instructional leadership problems encountered over many years of coaching school leaders. The stories are about different K–12 schools and include both administrators and teachers as instructional leaders. The framework components for each success story are briefly described below:

Instructional Leadership Challenge: This section pinpoints the main challenge facing the instructional leader. It gives the reader just enough background information for a basic understanding of the situation and provides the context of the success story.

Coaching Point: This section reveals the key coaching point and includes some of the questions asked of the instructional leader during the time of the coaching experience. The coaching point helps the instructional leader to think through the challenge with an eye toward a possible leadership response. The coaching aim is to encourage reflection in action.

Instructional Leadership Approach: This section is the most comprehensive. It describes the strategies and techniques used to overcome the instructional leadership challenge and help close the teaching gap. In some stories, specifics such as a collaborative protocol or particular method of inquiry will be included to increase the take-away value of the success story.

Results: This section explains what happened and the impact of the instructional leadership approach on teaching and learning. Postreflections from the instructional leaders are also included. This section is mainly for understanding and to reinforce the essential practices that can improve instructional leadership (see table above).

Extension: This section provides an opportunity to extend the impact of effective instructional leadership through reflections and connections with your own work as an instructional leader.

Theory of Action: The if/then statement that connects the leader's overall leadership strategy to the actions and relationships critical to success as an instructional leader. It is the why, what, and how of leading for success.

Success Story #1: Learning How to Work as a Team

Instructional Leader: Fifth-grade-level chair

Time Period: Six months

Instructional Leadership Challenge: The biggest challenge leading this grade-level team was the lack of collaboration and the motivation to work as a cohesive group. The teachers were experienced and very independent. Nothing much was ever accomplished together. Many meetings were met with negativity, especially when the grade chair had to present test data from the building principal. In this particular situation, the principal had asked each 3–6 grade-level team to analyze the reasons why 33% of the elementary students were having difficulty with problem-solving, especially with extended-response items (open-ended questions). Some of the fifth-grade teachers felt that the problem was how math was being taught in the lower grades. Other teachers believed that the new math program did not adequately cover problem-solving. A few teachers were reluctant to share their opinions.

Coaching Point: The principal's request to look at student problem-solving might be just the context for addressing the problem the team has with collaboration. Think of a time when you were a part of a team of teachers who worked well together on an instructional matter. What structures were in place to support collaboration? How did the leader get everyone involved?

Instructional Leadership Approach:

- Scheduled the first meeting when the team would have more time (2 hours). The purpose was to look at samples of students' problem-solving work with extended response items taken from previous state Grade 5 math tests, and *together,* analyze where students were having the most difficulty. Samples of student work (names removed) were sent out in advance.
- Facilitated the meeting using a three-round collaborative protocol. Round one had teachers in groups of three. Each teacher had 5 minutes to present her analysis without discussion or interruption. In round two, each small group had to develop a three-point diagnostic assessment of student problem-solving. Round three brought everyone back together to share their findings. The grade chair served as recorder, and the teachers took turns as presenters.
- Compiled the group diagnostic and sent it out to all fifth-grade teachers and the principal the next day.
- A series of three follow-up grade-level meetings were held. The focus at each meeting was on how to improve problem-solving skills.

Results: The fifth-grade teachers worked together using the collaborative analysis to guide needed changes in teaching problem-solving. Several new teaching methods were included in their plan: (1) students would be given examples of well-written extended responses from a student file and asked to identify why they were good; (2) students would be given more time in class to struggle with extended response math problems before the teachers would intercede; and (3) students would be encouraged to share their problem-solving strategies during *talk-alouds* with classmates. During the months that followed, there was evidence from homework assignments and formative assessments that students were improving their extended responses.

Postreflections from the fifth-grade level chair:

- ✓ She felt that the 2-hour meeting was one of the best meetings she ever facilitated. Finally, the teachers were working together. The preparation, extended time, and use of a protocol that allowed all voices to be heard made the difference.
- ✓ The immediate follow-up gave the teachers an opportunity to try some of the new methods, learn from each other, and work on teaching methods that were important for their students.
- ✓ Not every grade-level meeting was perfect after that, but there was a definite increase in the motivation to work as a cohesive group.

Extension: Disjointed grade-level or department meetings undermine the collaboration and cohesiveness needed to make substantial instructional improvements. This grade-level chair made good use of assessment information that was real for teachers—student work. Instead of concentrating on the percentage of students who were experiencing difficulty with problem-solving, the grade chair put the focus on the teaching methods used and not on the competency of the teachers. This opened the door to greater teacher participation, which helped these fifth-grade teachers change methods where students were not succeeding.

Theory of Action: If I can involve the teachers in something that they feel is important for their students, then I have a much better chance in helping them to collaborate as a team to make needed changes in their teaching methods.

Success Story #2: Increasing Graduation Rates: Plan for Success

Instructional Leader: High school assistant principal, Grades 9–12

Time Period: 12 months

Instructional Leadership Challenge: The assistant principal supervised the four core academic, special education, and counseling department chairs in a low-performing high school. His biggest challenge was given to him by the principal—to increase graduation rates by coordinating an initiative (Plan for Success—PfS) that targets struggling ninth-grade students and places them in a cohort with master teachers. The goal was to make sure that these students stayed in school with the skills, knowledge, and attitudes needed to be successful. According to the principal, this was to be the assistant principal's number-one assignment for the upcoming school year.

Coaching Point: This is a complex initiative with a number of complicated interrelated variables. Draw a diagram that connects everyone who is affected by this PfS initiative and think of the implications these relationships have for targeting struggling ninth graders. Use this patterned thinking approach to develop your instructional leadership plan and strategies. What will it take for the PfS team to be successful? How will the principal be involved? What about the high school faculty? What changes will you need to make in your own work?

Instructional Leadership Approach:

May and June

- The PfS initiative got underway the last 2 months of the school year when the assistant principal met with the principal and six department chairs to lay out the PfS.
- The principal was updated during weekly meetings with the assistant principal.

Over the summer

- The chair of the counseling department and the eighth-grade school counselor identified 25 incoming ninth graders who were struggling academically, had a history of school-related problems, and were at risk for possible failure or dropping out of school. Five were put on a waiting list. The target group would include 15 general education students and five special education students.

- The science, math, English, social studies, and special education department chairs identified a master teacher in their department who would teach the targeted classes. In some cases, the master teacher was the department chair.
- The PfS team was composed of the assistant principal, department chairs, and master teachers. Ten members.
- Spent 3 days with the department chairs and master teachers developing the cohort intervention program. This included establishing a shared understanding of student-centered learning, curriculum modifications, special education consulting teacher model, opportunities for tutoring, parental/home involvement, formative assessments, electronic progress reports, bimonthly team meetings, and a dedicated communication system for the PfS team.
- The chair of the counseling department developed a support program that would offer individual and group services to the targeted students. Support program increased contact time with students and parents/guardians.
- Modified the daily bell schedule so that all members of the PfS team could eat lunch together and were free of teaching duties the last two periods on Friday afternoons.

September to June

- Introduced the PfS team and the program for the 20 targeted ninth-grade students at the first faculty meeting. Faculty members were invited to ask questions.
- The five PfS teachers ate lunch together every day. Used this time to discuss students and address problems.
- Met with the PfS team every Friday afternoon for 80 minutes. The agenda was always the same, the learning progress of the 20 students in the cohort and an exchange of successful teaching methods and conditions of learning. When possible, teachers integrated learning across several curricular areas. Classroom observations, formative assessments, student work, and effort were the basis of the electronic progress reports.

- The chair of the counseling department met with each student and parent/guardian at least once during each semester. PfS students could request additional counseling at any time. The counselor met frequently with groups of students with similar needs.
- Received a daily attendance report for the targeted students and provided immediate follow-up with parents/guardians. Handled all of the discipline problems for the cohort.
- Updated principal at weekly meetings and the entire faculty at monthly meetings.
- Two students opted out of the PfS program and were replaced with two students from the waiting list.

Preliminary Results: After the first year, 16 PfS students passed ninth grade and their four academic courses. The other four students earned needed credits at summer school. The interdisciplinary team functioned like a true team. The PfS team was given a specific charge and allowed to design the program and select the teaching methods that they believed were best for the students (e.g., increased use of computer-based diagnostic teaching). There is every reason to believe that this intervention plan will help struggling students make it through their first year of high school.

Postreflections from the assistant high school principal:

- ✓ Felt the combination of excellent teaching and the conditions that allowed the team to function as a team (e.g., time for team meetings, lunch together, and a dedicated system of communication) made this intervention program work. Without support conditions in place, it is doubtful if the initiative would have been so successful.
- ✓ Communication with the faculty was important. Despite the success, some teachers felt the PfS team was being given special consideration. These feelings were addressed.
- ✓ Nervous about designating teachers as master teachers. Having the department chairs involved in this process helped a great deal.

Extension: There is much to be learned about how schools are organized for student success. Teachers and instructional leaders often are working with their hands tied behind their backs because there are so many constraints that get in the way of optimal teaching and learning. Assistant principal built the PfS around a shared vision of student-centered learning and the need to schedule time for teachers to work collaboratively. Those two factors were culture changers for the high school teachers involved. Assistant principal modified leadership responsibilities in two distinct ways: (1) provided a great deal more of face-to-face time with everyone involved and (2) trusted the teachers to take the responsibility for helping these struggling students make it through ninth grade—one important step to earning a high school diploma prepared for the next stage of their lives.

Theory of Action: If I want teachers to be more proactive, then I need to work with the teachers to develop a shared vision of learning and provide the conditions needed to support their efforts, for example, time to meet.

Success Story #3: Team Learns More About Teaching

Instructional Leader: Third-grade-level chair

Time Period: Five months

Instructional Leadership Challenge: At the beginning of the school year, the elementary principal asked each grade-level team to pick one area of teaching to study together. In addition to the scheduled weekly, 40-minute grade-level meetings, the principal added a half-day conference in October that could be used as part of the study. At the end of January, each grade-level team would share the results of their study at a second, half-day conference. The study initiative was not about raising test scores; it was about improving teaching methods. After years of concentrating on reading and math, the third-grade team decided to study science teaching. The challenge for the third-grade-level chair was how to facilitate a 4-month study of science teaching.

Coaching Point: This challenge opened the door to a unique opportunity for the third-grade teachers to learn more about teaching together. Without the usual pressure to raise test scores, the teachers could concentrate on their own professional learning. How can you capitalize on this opportunity to learn together? How will you and the teachers find time to do this?

Instructional Leadership Approach:

- The first two third-grade team meetings were devoted to developing a plan for learning more about science teaching. Invited the middle school and high school science department chairs to attend these two planning sessions. Asked teachers to think about the conditions that mattered the most to them as learners (e.g., time to learn together). Those were the conditions that she would try to establish for them.
- With the guidance of the science department chairs, the teachers developed a list of doable study activities to implement together over the next 4 months:
  o Develop questions to guide the study of teaching science.
  o Read the National Science Teachers Association's (NSTA) two-page Position Statement on Teaching Elementary Science.
  o View a 30-minute introductory NSTA Web Seminar on teaching elementary science.
  o Participate in a half-day science workshop (facilitated by a knowledgeable science educator).
  o Observe two exemplar videotaped science lessons.
  o With a partner, develop and teach one science lesson based on new learning.
  o Devote 30 minutes of every grade-level meeting to science teaching.
- Developed a 4-month schedule of team meetings with topics devoted to each one of the study activities. Most activities took two meetings.
- Facilitated the development of the questions that would guide the study of science teaching. For example: What does research say about teaching elementary science? What aspects of our science curriculum are in line with this thinking? What changes will need to be made?
- Worked with the science department chairs and the regional science director to find someone to facilitate the half-day workshop in October. The person chosen was an elementary science teacher from a nearby school district.

- Facilitated team viewing and discussing multimedia inquiry-based science lessons.
- Asked teachers to keep a journal during the 4-month study, and teachers occasionally referenced their journal entries during a grade-level meeting.
- Did everything possible to reduce the time needed to handle routine organizational matters. The 10-minute limit on nonscience discussions was strictly enforced at each grade-level meeting.

Results: The third-grade teachers learned a lot about teaching science and gradually developed a vision statement for teaching science. Inquiry science with first-hand exploration and investigation was the basis of the vision statement. Many teachers purchased resource books on inquiry-based science teaching and shared ideas and lesson suggestions with colleagues. The third-grade report to the faculty in January was mostly demonstrations of inquiry-based science teaching. The department chair received permission from the principal for the teachers to visit a nearby elementary school where the workshop facilitator taught. It was known to have an exemplary elementary science program. During the last 5 months of school, the grade chair made time at team meetings for teachers to update each other about their science teaching. Some teachers even found a way to observe in each other's classrooms.

Postreflections from the third-grade-level chair:

- ✓ The third-grade chair spoke highly of the principal's decision to ask his teachers to learn more about teaching. She doubted if it would have happened without his instructional leadership.
- ✓ She wanted to model professional learning in the same way that was best for teaching elementary science—through collaborative inquiry. The conditions for learning more about science teaching, for example, using questions to guide investigations, were the same kinds of conditions that would work best for students learning science. Experience is a good teacher.
- ✓ Never realized that teachers had never watched the same lessons together. This experience led to some of our best discussions about teaching science.

✓ It was best not to bite off more than the teachers could chew. The inquiry activities were doable because they were within the time and schedule constraints found in the school.

Extension: At least during this 4-month study, the culture of teaching for these third-grade teachers changed. Contemporary psycholinguist Frank Smith used to say when asked about teaching students to think: "Do not teach students to think, give them something to think about." That same logic applies to helping teachers learn more about teaching. The benefit of teachers learning more about teaching through their own work as professionals surpassed anything they could learn from a more traditional approach to improving methods. The real work of the third-grade chair was ahead as she works with the teachers to implement inquiry-based science teaching. This grade chair was already thinking of ways to facilitate and support teachers moving forward with a better way for students to learn science.

Theory of Action: If I want teachers to learn more about teaching, then I have to help them to learn from the process itself and not simply by looking for best practice.

Success Story #4: Learning to Lead Learning

Instructional Leader: Assistant superintendent for instruction

Time Period: Ten months

Instructional Leadership Challenge: The district established two leadership teams, Grades K–6 and 7–12. Both leadership teams were led by the assistant superintendent for instruction and met separately every month during the school year. The challenge for the assistant superintendent was to build the capacity of the district's school leaders to work together to improve student achievement (i.e., lead learning). She wanted them to learn together.

Coaching Point: Effective leadership is vital to the success of a school. Research and practice confirm that there is slim chance of creating and sustaining high-quality learning environments without skilled and committed leaders (administrators and teachers) to help shape teaching and learning. How can you build on the knowledge and skills of these leaders? How would you focus each 90-minute monthly meeting to maximize learning that would strengthen instructional leadership?

Instructional Leadership Approach:

- Developed a four-part meeting structure that would be used throughout the year:
  - Start each meeting with an instructional leadership success story. How are you using what you are learning? (10 minutes)
  - View a 10-minute teaching episode and discuss the teaching and evidence of learning (30 minutes).
  - Discuss one of the 7 Disciplines for Strengthening Instruction* from the Harvard Change Leadership Group (30 minutes).
  - Address one problem of practice related to improving instructional leadership (20 minutes).

---

*Summarized on page 123.

- Used this meeting format throughout the school year.
- Looked for evidence that the school leaders were using what they were learning together in their work as instructional leaders.

Results: The capacity of the two leadership teams to work together to improve student achievement was not only noticeable during meeting times from discussions about problems of practice, it was evident that the school leaders were applying what they were learning on-the-job in their respective schools.

Postreflections from the assistant superintendent for instruction:

- ✓ Felt this experience was the first time she ever sustained leadership development that was so closely connected to improving and shaping teaching and learning.
- ✓ The feedback from the school leaders themselves and staff indicated that the leadership development was making a difference in their effectiveness as instructional leaders.

✓ Perhaps the single greatest accomplishment of the group was the development of a widely shared vision of what is good teaching, one of the Disciplines for Strengthening Instruction.

Extension: When education leaders work together to deepen their understanding of leading learning, the entire district benefits. Just as instructional leaders work with teachers to change methods where students are not succeeding, school leaders must work together to change methods where instructional leadership is not succeeding. Instructional leadership that is aligned across all schools and grade levels holds the promise for being the most effective in improving teaching and learning.

Theory of Action: If I want school leaders to become more involved as instructional leaders, then I have to facilitate a process that is grounded by effective instructional leadership practice—model the behaviors and actions that I expect.

Success Story #5: Test Prep and Instruction

Instructional Leader: Middle school principal, Grades 6–8

Time Period: Ten months

Instructional Leadership Challenge: The middle school principal's greatest challenge was helping teachers to design better learning opportunities for students. She wanted to see students develop as independent learners. Instead, she was seeing more lessons where the teachers did most of the thinking, most of the talking, and often, most of the work. Despite the fact that student scores on state assessments had increased the past 2 years, many lessons were still aimed at preparing students for tests. She was worried that the pressure to improve student achievement had finally found its way into the decisions teachers were making about which methods to use.

Coaching Point: Effective teachers carefully plan their instruction and make choices about which methods to use based on how students learn best (decision points). Teachers who are worried about test results may choose methods and strategies for a different reason. How can you approach such a sensitive subject as a teacher's choice of methods? How do the teachers feel about the methods they are using? Is pressure to improve student achievement part of the problem? Are there ways to influence teachers' decision points of instructional planning?

Instructional Leadership Approach: Phase 1

- Talked individually with several teacher leaders in the building, including the grade and department chairs, to find out how teachers were feeling about the instructional methods they were using. Most believed that they and the teachers were spending a lot more time preparing students for tests and that some student-centered methods such as inquiry-based learning and project work were not being used as much. More attention was given to teaching students strategies to improve performance on the increasing number of formative and summative assessments.
- Met with the superintendent and assistant superintendent for instruction to explain what she was planning on doing with the staff.
- At the October faculty meeting, the principal informed the staff that she would be meeting with each teacher individually to talk about the impact increased testing was having on their selection of teaching methods and instruction in general. These conversations would not be part of the annual professional performance review process.
- Individual meetings were held with each teacher during October, November, and December.

Results from Phase 1: The principal learned that most teachers were indeed frustrated by the amount of time spent preparing students for tests and analyzing the results. They believed that instructional time had been reduced due to testing and that their decisions about which methods to use were frequently compromised by how well students were doing on tests. Some teachers even reported that they had discontinued some unit projects for lack of instructional time. On the plus side, many teachers felt that the formative assessments did inform their teaching and helped them to zero in on the needs of students.

Postreflections from the principal:

- ✓ There is a need to find a balance between sustaining increased student achievement on the state assessments and the need for more student-centered teaching and learning.
- ✓ Although the teachers and I cannot change the system of standardized testing, we might be able to change how we fit into that system.

Instructional Leadership Approach: Phase 2

- At the first faculty meeting in January, teachers discussed how testing was affecting instruction and instructional time. Each table had a mix of Grades 6, 7, and 8 teachers.
- Asked teachers to continue these discussions at the February and March grade- and department-level meetings. Recommendations would be developed around two guiding questions: (1) What steps can we take to prepare students for assessments without compromising student-centered teaching and learning? (2) How can we help students become better independent learners?

Results from Phase 2: Below is a summary of the best recommendations from grade and department teachers presented at the April faculty meeting:

- Do not alter student-centered teaching methods to accommodate standardized tests. Instead, use a balanced mix of assessment information to strengthen instructional planning by integrating test preparation into lessons. For example, teaching science students to understand and know how to apply scientific knowledge, rather than just memorize.
- Increase the use of strategy instruction, especially to address deficiencies identified with formative assessments. More modeling, demonstrations, and shared and guided practice that enable students to improve independent strategies needed for success with all types of learning, including success on standardized tests.
- Teach students how to be independent. Challenge students to stand on their own as thinkers and learners.
- When it comes time for test prep, help students see that instruction throughout the unit has been preparing them for state or district assessments.

- Spread out the concept of review games across a marking period using modified homework assignments, daily warm-ups, and out-the-door questions.
- Increase student-directed activities aimed at helping each other learn difficult skills and concepts. One way is forming in-class study clubs.
- We cannot change the system, but we can change the way we approach the system.

Postreflections from the principal:

✓ Classroom observations the remainder of the school year provided evidence that the teachers were trying to implement some of the recommendations.
✓ The change in perspective, from reactive to proactive, made all the difference.

Extension: Designing better learning opportunities for students sometimes means creating better learning opportunities for teachers (i.e., critical learning opportunities). The principal did not have the solution to the testing dilemma, but she was wise enough to share instructional leadership with all of the teachers. This success story reinforces why an instructional leader needs to make it safe for teachers to openly discuss an issue that is normally discussed privately. The pressure associated with raising test scores can sometimes undermine the very methods that the teachers and administrators believe are best for students.

Theory of Action: If I want teachers to take greater responsibility for improving teaching, then I sometimes have to step out of their way, let teachers do it their way, and support their efforts in the process.

Success Story #6: Coaching Teachers

Instructional Leader: Elementary principal, Grades K–5

Time Period: Three years

Instructional Leadership Challenge: The district received a 3-year Science, Technology, Engineering, and Mathematics (STEM) federal grant. Part of the money could be used to add two full-time coaching positions in the K–5 elementary school. The STEM goal at the elementary school was to improve the teaching of science. STEM coaches were not allowed to provide direct services to students. Current staff was encouraged to apply for the coaching positions, but no one did. The two coaches hired were experienced teachers and instructional coaches. One coach was assigned to Grades K–2 and the other coach to Grades 3–5. The principal's greatest challenge was how to get the teachers involved in the planning and implementation of a coaching program as full participants.

Coaching Point: Teachers had no prior experience working with an instructional coach. To be effective, the coaching program would need to be planned and developed by the teachers and coaches with as much upfront involvement as possible. The principal's greatest challenge was facilitating a planning and implementation process that would result in effective in-class coaching. What concerns do you think the teachers will have about a coaching program? How do you see your role as principal throughout this process? How can you support the invitational value of coaching?

Instructional Leadership Approach:

- May-June faculty meetings. All teachers involved in preliminary discussions about the coaching program. Expectations for teachers and coaches were a part of those discussions. The goal was to develop a 3-year coaching plan aimed at improving the teaching of science. The 3-year plan would include a job description for coaches, guidelines for teacher participation, science curriculum and methods study, evaluation plan, and a 30-minute monthly meeting for coaches and teachers at each grade level.
- The 3-year draft plan written over the summer by a team, which included the principal, teachers representing each grade level, middle and high school science department chairs, and the two science coaches. The plan laid out a steady progression of teacher involvement over the next 3 years.
- September-October faculty meetings. Teachers and coaches reviewed the 3-year draft plan addressing misunderstandings and making needed changes or revisions. The plan was unanimously approved by the teachers.

- ○ Coaches spent the first 2 months getting to know the teachers, visiting classrooms, reviewing the science curriculum, helping teachers with their long-range science planning, and working out flexible schedules for grade-level meetings.
- ○ Principal met with teachers and science coaches as much as possible throughout the 3 years.

Results: Year 1 was devoted mostly to planning science lessons and building on methods teachers were already using to teach science. As the year went by, teachers and coaches were meeting on a regular basis in small groups or by grade level to talk about science instruction. Many teachers requested demonstration lessons, which were a part of the Year 1 plan. Highlights of the first year of science coaching were presented at the end-of-year faculty meeting. Year 2 was devoted to mostly in-class support and individual and small-group coaching sessions. Science coaches worked alongside teachers and also provided feedback after observing a lesson. All teachers had at least two 30-minute periods a month to meet with their coach. Year 3 continued the coaching sessions and in-class support, but more attention was given to developing methods to address areas of student deficiencies (e.g., summarizing findings). Local and state assessments were used to pinpoint student needs. Teachers would often work together developing new methods. The evaluation of student achievement was compiled by the principal and shared with the faculty. The results were very positive in terms of increased student learning, development of effective methods, and the confidence teachers had acquired as science teachers.

Postreflections from the principal:

- ✓ This plan would have never worked without all of the teachers being involved. Teachers were given time and support to adjust to a coaching experience.
- ✓ Teacher collaboration never higher. Teachers continue to coach each other sharing ideas and providing constructive feedback.

Extension: This principal understood change leadership. He knew that coaching was perceived by all teachers as a second-order change. The principal provided the extra face-to-face communication, shared decision-making, and in-class support needed to help teachers improve their science teaching. Realistic expectations were set so teachers could deepen their understanding of science teaching and learning. The teaching methods were not superimposed; they were developed from the interactions between the teachers and the coaches. The students learned more because the methods teachers were using improved, helping them to learn how to apply what they knew.

Theory of Action: If I want to help teachers make desired instructional change, then I must be willing to change what I do as a leader to make that happen.

Success Story #7: Positive Impact of Collaboration and Peer Observations

Instructional Leader: High school math department chair, Grades 9–12

Time Period: Five months (one semester)

Instructional Leadership Challenge: Department teachers were comfortable dropping in on each other's classrooms but had never collaborated on lesson design or been a part of structured peer observations. The chair's greatest challenge was to support teachers taking a risk to improve their lessons and teaching methods and how to make the process more than just a collegial experience with no follow-up or effect on teaching practice.

Coaching Point: Teachers give lip service to the value of teamwork, but generally, most cultures of teaching provide very little evidence of true collaboration. The chance to design a lesson together followed by an opportunity for peer observations and feedback could help to raise the bar on instructional collaboration. How would you start with the department teachers, building on their positive interpersonal relationships? How can you facilitate and guide this collaborative process? What conditions must be in place in order for peer observations to work?

Instructional Leadership Approach:

- The district had been working on an initiative to improve lesson design across all grade levels and subject areas.

- Took time to discuss the components of a good lesson design at two department meetings. Each teacher shared ideas about the design components, and all agreed to participate in a modified lesson study that would include peer observations and constructive feedback about the lesson.
- Department chair went first, and together with two other geometry teachers, the study trio designed a lesson together.
- The department chair taught the lesson, and the two teachers received coverage for their classes so that they could observe the lesson.
- After the lesson, the study trio met to discuss the lesson and how it went. Feedback from teachers observing was used to improve the lesson, and it was taught again by one of the other teachers.
- Algebra and Algebra 2/Trigonometry teachers formed a study trio and repeated the same process as the one pioneered by the department chair.
- Teachers observing were asked to keep two things in mind as they watched the lesson: What worked for students? How could this lesson be improved?
- The results of both lessons were summarized and made available to every teacher in the department.
- Follow-up reports were on the agenda for the next two department meetings. There was much discussion about the value of this process and how it could be supported in the future.

Results: During the semester, every teacher in the math department taught one lesson with colleagues watching and observed one lesson and provided constructive feedback for at least one other teacher. The response from teachers was overwhelmingly positive. The experience was considered highly professional and led to a number of lesson modifications, and in two cases, a change in the method for reviewing homework with much greater involvement of students as teachers. Discussions at subsequent department meetings were often related to what the teachers had learned from peer observations.

Postreflections from the department chair:

✓ The ice had been broken. I need to capitalize on what happened with peer observations and collaborative lesson design.

✓ The teachers and I need to spend more time learning about teaching and thinking of ways we can improve our lessons and methods by working together.

✓ I need to get into classrooms more often.

Extension: Teachers are often unaware of how their colleagues teach. This type of isolation may in fact be a way of avoiding having to deal with issues of professional competency. Good teaching comes from seeing good teaching much the same way that a master teaching a class helps develop higher levels of ability in those not considered as proficient. When teachers open their classrooms to each other, it is a sign they are assuming greater responsibility for improving teaching methods.

Theory of Action: If the teachers and I learn more about teaching together from lesson collaboration and peer observations, then we are more apt to help each other improve teaching methods and solve instructional problems.

Success Story #8: Helping Students With Disabilities Meet Standards

Instructional Leader: Middle school assistant principal, Grades 6–8

Time Period: Ten months

Instructional Leadership Challenge: The middle school implemented a number of measures to increase student achievement (e.g., new learning center and extended tutoring services). Last year, eighth-grade students with disabilities did not meet adequate yearly progress (AYP) goals in English Language Arts (ELA), Mathematics, and Science; all other student groups made AYP. His greatest challenge was working with a variety of teachers and specialists to help students with disabilities meet standards and make AYP.

Coaching Point: Chart all the ways that students with disabilities receive instruction (e.g., 15–1 resource room). Next to each delivery system, write down if instruction is delivered by a special education teacher, general education teacher, or both. What are the implications of this chart for your instructional leadership practice? What adjustments, if any, will you need to make in your work as an instructional leader? What problems do you foresee?

Instructional Leadership Approach:

- Met with ELA, math, science, and special education department chairs. Asked them to put together a list of general and special education teachers at each grade level who share a common set of students with disabilities. These teachers would work together as a team to address the specific needs of the students with disabilities.
- Met with department chairs and each team of teachers by grade level. The first question asked was: What can we (assistant principal and department chairs) do to support your efforts to help students with disabilities make AYP?
- Established three essential functions for each team. (1) Use Individual Educational Plan (IEP) and subject-specific assessments to pinpoint what each student needs to know and be able to do in order to make adequate progress. (2) Meet once a week for 40 minutes to share information about how each student is doing. Time built into schedule. (3) Work together to develop effective teaching methods and strategies.
- Student progress monitored every 5 weeks by assistant principal and special education caseload managers.
- Met with each team four times during the first year.
- Problems were addressed immediately.

Results: The teams sought support in four main areas: (1) expectations for student work and assignments, (2) behavioral problems, (3) testing modifications, and (4) paperwork. General and special education teachers collaborated on curriculum, lesson planning, formative assessments, and teaching methods, strategies, and techniques. After the first year, students with disabilities made AYP in Language Arts and Mathematics using safe harbor target and made AYP in science.

Postreflections from the assistant principal:

- ✓ Teaming worked because there was a structure established to support ongoing communication and collaboration and resolve problems quickly.
- ✓ Although differences in teachers' expectations about students with disabilities did not disappear, there was much

less frustration on the part of general and special education teachers. For example, general education teachers
were not feeling as if they were *watering down* their teaching and curriculum.
✓ I learned how important it is to modify my leadership practices in order to support greater collaboration. I spent a lot
more time helping the teachers trust each other more.

Extension: The assistant principal made a critical choice at the
beginning of the school year to work closely with general and special education department chairs. Shared instructional leadership
was necessary to gain the cooperation of general and special education teachers. Students with special needs routinely work with a
number of teachers and specialists. This *medical model* has developed over many years. What has been missing is the ability to
coordinate the efforts of all of the professionals in the best interests of the students. That is the instructional leadership challenge.

Theory of Action: If I want to make sure all students make
AYP, then I have to make sure that the teachers and specialists
who work with non-AYP students have the direction and support
needed for effective collaboration.

Success Story #9: Increasing Mastery-Level Learning

Instructional Leader: High school principal, Grades 9–12

Time Period: Two years

Instructional Leadership Challenge: The goal was to increase
the number of high school students reaching mastery level (85%
or better) in four core academic areas as measured by local and
state assessments. The high school principal's greatest challenge
was helping Grades 9–12 teachers increase their understanding
and use of diagnostic teaching and small-group instruction.

Coaching Point: This is no ordinary challenge. You are talking
about affecting the teaching methods of many teachers. On the
plus side, this initiative is not about ineffective teachers, but rather
helping good teachers improve their methods. What are your concerns about the culture of teaching and the conditions of support

necessary for desired instructional change? Where is the logical place for you to begin? How will you convince teachers that there is a need to improve? Will anyone think that there will be a letdown at the other levels of progress, especially those students who are failing courses?

Instructional Leadership Approach:
Year 1

- Formed a School Improvement Team (SIT) made up of general and special education teachers, department chairs, school counselors, assistant principal, and herself. Mastery data from the previous 3 years were shared. The average percent of students who earned above an 85% in all four core academic areas was 24%. The goal was to bring this percentage up to an average of 40% by the end of 2 years.
- Used a common template to guide discussions and action, every department was asked to describe what it takes for a student to reach mastery level in their subject area and to develop an action plan to share with SIT. The plan must contain at least four common elements: (1) an ongoing assessment and analysis of student needs and progress; (2) evidence of diagnostic teaching (look at curriculum with a new lens); (3) evidence of how small-group instruction will be incorporated; and (4) two new department initiatives to support the goal of increased mastery (e.g., looking at student work collaboratively or forming a study group to improve methods).
- Action Plans reviewed by SIT with constructive feedback to strengthen them.
- Support conditions would include a small stipend for professional development and resources, a half-time substitute to share between departments to help facilitate peer observations or in-depth lesson study, and time set aside at every SIT meeting to share ideas and strategies that were having a positive impact on increasing mastery-level learning.
- Facilitated discussions with students in every class about master-level learning. Students more involved in formative assessments and goal setting.
- Ongoing progress reports and updates at monthly SIT meetings.

- Principal, assistant principal, and department chairs increased the amount of time they spent visiting classrooms and talking with the teachers in their classrooms.
- End-of-year reflections from each department and SIT members were compiled into a Report of Progress on Mastery-Level Learning and given to each teacher to read over the summer.

Year 2

- New department initiatives included extending and refining instructional planning and strategies across all departments and grade levels, senior enrichment program, innovations with technology-based learning (e.g., computerized problem-solving, simulations, and higher level thinking games), addition of science and math clubs, rebirth of school newspaper, team projects in all subjects, early intervention program from school counselors (e.g., study techniques, grade awareness, academic engagement, and improvement plans), a teacher and student joint project emerged entitled: Innovation and Design for the Future, and AP student study teams.
- Increased face-to-face communication with staff.
- Highlighted mastery-level initiatives at faculty meetings and in weekly staff newsletter.
- Student learning achievements displayed around school and in the community on equal footing as sports and other extracurricular accomplishments.

Results: The mastery level of high school students increased and reached the goal of 40% by the end of the second year. The percentages of students passing the core academic subjects also increased during this period. Teachers took greater responsibility for improving their teaching methods and shared ideas and strategies that worked well. Diagnostic teaching, that is, teaching based on the needs of students rather than on the content that must be covered, slowly became part of the culture of teaching at the high school as well as a more favorable attitude about peer observations. Small-group instruction was no longer the exception, and teachers were finding a balance between whole- and small-group learning. Students were given more opportunities to apply classroom learning and skills in ongoing school-based projects and organizations,

Extension: Something good always happens when teachers pull together for the same purpose and when that purpose is important for students and staff. The principal knew that the best way for teachers to improve their methods—diagnostic teaching and small-group instruction—was by having them work together on increasing mastery-level learning and by sharing strategies and ideas that worked. The struggle to create better learning opportunities for students often leads to innovation and greater use of creativity. This success story reinforces the value of students and teachers working together to improve teaching and learning.

Theory of Action: If I want to increase mastery-level learning for students, then I must support the conditions needed for mastery-level learning for teachers. It appears you cannot have one without the other.

Success Story #10: The Power of Innovation: Leading by Example:

The last success story is slightly different from the others. There is no specific instructional leader, just a group of music educators trying to learn more about teaching from each other. It reinforces how important collaborative inquiry is to improving methods. As you read this story, think about the power of innovation to influence desired instructional change. This success story is all about teachers leading themselves and connects many practices associated with effective instructional leadership.

Background Information: Every summer, 25 band directors from all over the state are invited to attend the Oatka Instrumental Music Institution (OIMI) for a 2-week music symposium. In addition to the band directors, 200 outstanding student musicians in Grades 4–12 are also invited to attend the OIMI Symposium. The students receive a superb program of individualized instruction and become part of at least one performing group. These students learn from the teaching artists at the symposium right along with the music educators. The OIMI Symposium is an *experiment in learning* that combines both students and teachers as learners.

Instructional Leaders: Band directors

Instructional Leadership Challenge: During the 2006 summer OIMI Symposium, a group of seven band directors were asked to observe the other 18 directors while they were rehearsing their select bands. The purpose was to analyze the teaching and directing techniques and to synthesize their findings into a collection of effective methods that could be shared with band directors across the state.

Coaching Point: These music educators needed no coaching. They realized how important it was for teachers and students to learn from each other.

Instructional Leadership Approach:

- The seven band director/observers used an observational guide sheet that had been developed specifically for use at the OIMI Symposium. One category was titled "Innovative Techniques." Observers were encouraged to pay special attention to possible innovations and were each given a video camera to record any aspect of a rehearsal method that they believed should be seen by all of the other band directors. Observations were conducted during rehearsals with each of the select bands.
- One of the directors was using a rehearsal method that none of the seven observers had ever seen before. When working on a particularly difficult piece of music, he would divide his student musicians into smaller groups of six or seven players. Each group was comprised of a balance of woodwind, brass, and percussion instruments. The director would ask each group to go off somewhere to rehearse a certain section of the piece. He told his student players to listen carefully to the music coming from the instruments other than their own. When the groups returned to the full band rehearsal, the students were expected to share what they had learned about playing the piece by listening to other instruments.
- The seven observers could not believe what they saw and heard when the full rehearsal got underway. Group-by-group the student musicians shared how listening to others had helped them to play better together. They talked about paying more attention to tempo, melody, and harmony,

different volume levels, and other dynamics that make a band tighter. These insights were carried over into the full band rehearsal and the observers noted a noticeable improvement in how the piece was played.

Results: The rehearsal method became the talk of the OIMI Symposium. So much so that the director was asked to give a special presentation to the entire group of music educators and students. That summer changed the way some band directors rehearsed their bands and how some students practiced their music. The small group or ensemble rehearsing technique is still in use today and is considered by many music teachers and band directors to be a very effective method.

Extension: The OIMI Symposium leaders understood how valuable it is for teachers and students to learn from each other. What is rare, however, is that both the band directors and the student musicians were learners together. This point is often missed when instructional leaders work with teachers to improve teaching methods. Students are seldom involved in the improvement process. The symposium organizers recognized the fact that much can be learned about improving teaching (or directing a band) when the skills and techniques are pulled from the teaching/ learning process itself. Rehearsals, like classroom teaching, are usually done behind closed doors. At the Symposium, those doors were opened to other professionals as a source of extended learning. When classrooms are private, the methods used in those classrooms are private.

Theory of Action: If we give educators more opportunities to try things differently, then we just might begin to understand how innovations in education are created.

WHEN IS GOOD INSTRUCTIONAL LEADERSHIP GOING ON?

When viewed as a whole, these stories expose common ground for fostering exemplary instructional leadership practices. What comes through these scenarios more than anything else is "how" instructional leaders go about their work. How things are done is just as important to success as what is being done.

Whenever teachers are given time during the day to work on school improvement, good instructional leadership is going on. Improvement work cannot be done on the fly. In each success story, the instructional leaders did everything possible to make sure that time was scheduled and protected for teachers to work together. It cannot be overstated how important time is to the success of an instructional initiative.

Whenever there is an increase of face-to-face communication with teachers, good instructional leadership is going on. Instructional leaders must triple their efforts to make sure that teachers are clear about the why, what, and how of an improvement effort. Confused teachers do not produce effective results. Emails and other electronic messaging systems may work well for announcements, agendas, and reports, but they are not sufficient to clarify misunderstandings or to resolve critical differences or problems.

Whenever teachers are receiving ongoing support in a timely and useful fashion, good instructional leadership is going on. Once teachers begin work on some aspect of improving teaching and learning they need ongoing in-class and general support to help them achieve their goals. Effective instructional leaders realize that teachers are not always able to make the decisions needed to move forward with an improvement project. Instructional leaders in the success stories all provided the conditions of support needed by teachers to achieve their goals.

Whenever teachers are using the classroom as the basis for learning more about teaching, good instructional leadership is going on. Teachers who watch each other teach and discuss what they are learning, look at student work collaboratively, and observe and talk with students about how they are learning will deepen their understanding of teaching and learning and put them on the right path to developing better methods. In many of the success stories, the classroom was the basis of improved professional learning for teachers.

Whenever teachers are able to carry out improvement efforts on their own, good instructional leadership is going on. The responsibility for improving teaching methods should rest with the teachers themselves. Years of misguided professional development and top-down thinking about school improvement has greatly diminished how teachers adapt to meet the needs of the students whom they serve. The success stories revealed just the opposite. Good instructional leaders help teachers gain back confidence in their own abilities to improve teaching methods.

Whenever teachers and teacher leaders are given the opportunity to help lead desired instructional change, good instructional leadership is going on. Many of the success stories revealed how principals and assistant principals joined forces with teacher leaders. These administrators were not reluctant to honor the leadership that rightly belongs to teachers or to establish structures that allowed teachers as instructional leaders to work more effectively with peers. Thinking administrators know that their strength as an instructional leader is compounded when they can truly collaborate with teacher leaders.

Whenever leadership practices and responsibilities are modified according to the magnitude of change perceived by the teachers, good instructional leadership is going on. Good instructional leaders never take desired change lightly. They find out all they can about how desired instructional change will affect the teachers. This does not mean that they give in to early signs of resistance, but rather, they come to understand it better so they can make leadership adjustments that will result in greater success. Shifts in practice, such as problem-based learning, are recognized and celebrated.

Whenever the learning experiences of the teachers are being facilitated and guided, good instructional leadership is going on. Success comes when teachers, responding to the learning needs of their students, discover ways to improve their teaching methods. Collaborative inquiry led by good instructional leaders replaces trendy programs or borrowed approaches deemed to be best practice. There is a belief that teacher learning can improve student learning.

Whenever teacher and administrative leaders reflect on what they are doing, good instructional leadership is going on. A reflective practice opens the door to better decision-making, thinking in action, and learning from mistakes. The fast-paced world of an education leader often blurs the need to think about what he is doing, but more importantly, how he is doing it. That is what makes reflection such a friend of instructional leadership. The instructional leaders in each success story used personal reflection as a source of professional growth and understanding.

- To learn how to improve teaching requires teachers to leave their classrooms—to attend professional development; to dialogue with colleagues about best practice; to share what is working and what is not working with colleagues; to observe best practice in other classrooms; to be a part of a working professional learning community.
- In my mind, the ideal situation would be a continual cycle of teachers learning new strategies, methods, and so on, through the means described above, practicing them in their own classrooms, and then having opportunities for reflection and feedback substantiated by evidence (student learning) on how the lessons went. ~ Bill

LEVERAGE YOUR STRENGTHS: X'S AND O'S

Read the coaching points for each instructional leadership practice found in Table 8.1. Put an "X" next to each point that you consider a strength of your current instructional leadership practice. Your decision to mark an "X" must be guided by your ability to think of evidence that demonstrates that the coaching point is part of your practice. Put an "O" next to each coaching point that you need to work on. When you have finished this self-assessment, think of how you can use your strengths to improve as an instructional leader. For instance, your insights about the culture of teaching are an asset when you are attempting to facilitate change where students are not succeeding.

Table 8.1   Core of Instructional Leadership Practices Recognized as Exemplary

Instructional Leadership Practices	X / O	Coaching Points to Consider
Increase your understanding of learning.		• Is your work grounded by research on how students learn?
		• Do you use the classroom as your laboratory for learning?
		• Do you observe students learning and talk with them about how they learn best?

Instructional Leadership Practices	X / O	Coaching Points to Consider
Ensure a widely shared vision of learning.		• Have you developed a vision of learning with teachers?
		• Do you use the vision to guide the instructional program from planning to delivery?
		• Do you look for evidence of the vision in daily practice and program development?
Get into classrooms as much as possible.		• Do you schedule classroom observations first?
		• Do you protect the time you have to be in classrooms?
		• Do you have a rock-solid plan for not being disturbed once you get into classrooms?
		• Are you keeping the monkeys off your back?
Help teachers learn more about teaching.		• Do you encourage innovation?
		• Do you value excellent teaching?
		• Do you schedule time for teams of teachers to work collaboratively?
		• Do you support this time with the resources and tools needed for professional inquiry?
		• Is teacher learning classroom-based?
Increase your understanding of the culture of teaching.		• Are you learning how your culture of teaching works by reflecting on successes and challenges?
		• Do you use what you learn to strengthen cooperation and address misconceptions and barriers?
Increase your understanding of change leadership.		• Do you determine the magnitude of change perceived by the teachers before you begin a new initiative?
		• Do you modify your instructional leadership according to the magnitude of change perceived by the teachers?

(Continued)

Table 8.1   (Continued)

Instructional Leadership Practices	X / O	Coaching Points to Consider
Work with teachers to change methods where students are not succeeding.		• Do you know what teaching methods are currently in use? *How* subjects are being taught?
		• Do you focus on *how* students are being asked to learn and not just on what they are learning?
		• Do you help teachers rethink their methods and not just consider what the students are or are not doing?
		• Do you know how master teachers make decisions about which methods to use?
Work with teachers to create better learning opportunities for students.		• Do teachers pinpoint why students are unsuccessful?
		• Does this analysis reach beyond student or home-related factors?
		• Does the analysis include looking at the methods and not just the data?
		• Are teachers being asked to rethink methods being used?
Use data to improve teaching.		• Do you and the teachers collect information about student learning from a variety of sources, especially classroom observations and student work?
		• Is this information transformed into improved methods?
Develop a theory of action.		• Do you help teachers to understand the what, the why, and the how of instructional improvement?
		• Do teachers have a theory of action perspective?
		• Do you have a theory of action perspective?
Strengthen shared instructional leadership.		• Do the teachers believe they are sharing instructional leadership?
		• Are you helping teacher leaders learn how to facilitate collaboration with their colleagues?
		• Are meetings models of collaboration and good teaching?

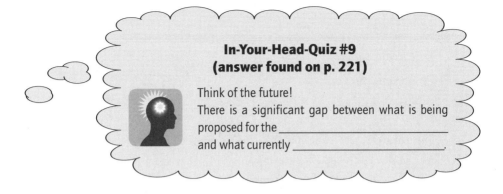

In-Your-Head-Quiz #9
(answer found on p. 221)

Think of the future!
There is a significant gap between what is being
proposed for the _____
and what currently _____.

INSTRUCTIONAL LEADERSHIP FOR THE 21ST CENTURY

"Although the responsibility of schools to educate students for communities and workplace has remained unchanged over the years, the communities and workplaces have changed.

21st Century education will require schools to teach less/learn more. The breadth and depth of proposed educational reform will exceed anything seen in the Effective Schools Movement of the 1980s and 1990s. The main components of schooling will include:

- Facilitated teams of globally linked students working on real problems
- Interwoven curriculum that connects core subjects with big ideas such as global awareness and civic, economic, and media literacy
- Teachers as facilitators of a learning environment
- Principals leading on-going instructional change

Nine practices of instructional leadership needed for the 21st Century:

1. Manage complexity

2. Leadership belief

3. Focus on change

4. Assesses needs

5. Leads learning

6. Facilitates changes

(Continued)

(Continued)

   7. Demonstrates relevancy

   8. Sets expectations

   9. Assesses progress

These nine practices are at work simultaneously, reiteratively, and randomly."

—Goslin (2010)

CLOSING THE TEACHING GAP

Instructional Leadership

"There is great variance in teachers' effectiveness in facilitating student learning."

—Curtis and Wurtzel, 2010 (p. 5)

Much of what this book advocates for in developing better instructional leaders can be translated into better learning opportunities for students. Unless conditions change, students will continue to do what they have been doing as long as teachers and administrators continue to do what they have been doing. What has changed, however, are achievement expectations for high school graduates—a primary source of motivation for closing the teaching gap.

A Look Back

To gain a better perspective about the future, let us look at the years 1990–2010 from two points of view: (1) the development of cellphones and (2) the development of teaching methods.

The cellphone industry reinvented itself many times over with the advent of 3G digital networks; smartphones with text, email, Internet access, streaming media, and third-party applications (apps); and unprecedented levels of connectivity, with more than two thirds of the U.S. population connected via cellphones.

During the same 20 years, teaching methods (especially the delivery of instruction) have been impacted by the increased use of modern technology (laptops, online learning, PowerPoint presentations, and interactive SMART Boards), but the methods are still mostly traditional and teacher directed. Promising methods like those used in project-based, inquiry-oriented, student-centered learning environments offered a glimmer of hope. Unfortunately, the ongoing pressure for greater accountability forced teachers and administrators to concentrate on improving tests results, not teaching methods. Just imagine if during these 20 years the kind of research and innovation that went into the development of cellphones had gone into the development of better learning opportunities for students.

This is not to say that individual teachers and schools are not improving teaching methods—they are—but it is difficult to identify improvements that are widespread. So, although some students benefit from better learning opportunities, those opportunities are not available to most students. To develop mastery, students need to be self-directed learners with the ability to apply what they know in ways that are meaningful, now and in the future. That type of learning requires a different type of teaching. One can only hope that President Barack Obama (November 4, 2009) will heed his own words, "It's time to stop just talking about education reform and start actually doing it. It's time to make education America's national mission."

The Way Forward

Do you think 21st-century learning can develop with current teaching methods? It must be that many civic, business, and political leaders think so because they rarely say a word about improving the teaching. The leaders like to talk about conceptual frameworks such as competing in the global economy, establishing labor-management collaborations, and, of course, the need for a comprehensive approach to reform (whatever that means). Will these well-intentioned frameworks help teachers teach better and students learn more?

One idea that I have had for a long time is the need to establish regional schools of innovation. Like the band directors in the last success story, teachers and students from different backgrounds and school types would come together over the summer, in partnership with nearby colleges of education, to learn how to improve teaching and learning. These schools could serve two purposes: (1) to provide a summer school experience for diverse populations of students and teachers and (2) to be an incubator for developing, researching, and sharing teaching methods that would ignite the joy of teaching and learning and prepare students for the 21st century. Methods developed at regional schools of innovation could be used to make sure that no urban student with a high school diploma would need to take remedial reading, writing, and mathematics in their first year of college. I see the teaching gap widening if the challenges of 21st-century education are addressed with business and political solutions rather than teaching and learning solutions.

As part of the American Recovery and Reinvestment Act (ARRA) signed into law on February 17, 2009, a competitive grant program, Race to the Top, was established with ambitious plans in four core education reform areas listed below. Please note that none of the goals is about improving teaching methods.

- Adopting standards and assessments that prepare students to succeed in college and the workplace and to compete in the global economy;
- Building data systems that measure student growth and success, and inform teachers and principals about how they can improve instruction;
- Recruiting, developing, rewarding, and retaining effective teachers and principals, especially where they are needed most; and
- Turning around our lowest-achieving schools.

In addition to these four goals, six priorities were established. It was no surprise that only one of the priorities contained the word *learning*: Priority 6: School-Level Conditions for Reform, Innovation, and Learning. Priority 6 might provide the best way forward in closing the teaching gap, but only if the invited innovation and conditions for learning focus on improving teaching methods.

Getting there, however, is not a scripted process, and do not look for a national effort to improve teaching. The real work to transform education will still need to be done at the classroom level by effective instructional leaders and creative teachers who have the ability to understand and interpret their school's culture of teaching, see the teaching and learning process for what it is, and have the courage to create better learning opportunities for students. That is the way forward.

TRY THIS: GIVE YOURSELF CREDIT

One of the main contentions in Chapter 8 is that when good instructional leadership is going on, there is a strong likelihood that the teaching gap will be narrowed, and in some cases, even closed.

Whether you are an emerging instructional leader or someone with years of experience, you need to take this opportunity to validate the good work that you do as an instructional leader.

Here's how, try THIS:

- Go to page 207 where it says, "What comes through these scenarios more than anything else is "how" instructional leaders go about their work."
- Re-read each of the nine practices considered examples of when good instructional leadership is going on.
- Use the scale below to rate yourself on each practice (do not be modest or overzealous in your ratings). Read each practice as if it were describing your work. I do this:

  1. All the time

  2. Sometimes

  3. Rarely

  4. Never

- How did you do?

The point here is that "how" you do your work is often just as important as what you do. Initially, your success as an instructional leader rests on reactions from the teachers and staff and the level to which they are willing to cooperate. Ultimately, however, your success as an instructional leader will rest on your ability to help teachers improve student learning.

LEADERSHIP TEAM ACTIVITY

Success Breeds Success

Purpose

Start with the end in mind.

- Each member of the leadership team will decide how a success story from the book can affect their own work and then together as a team, apply what they have learned from the experience to address a common instructional leadership challenge.
- Visualize the action needed to transfer seminar learning and understanding to current instructional leadership practice.

Perspective

- For some reason, educators are sometimes reluctant to embrace the success of others. Maybe it is because of the isolation found in the profession or a misguided feeling of competition. Whatever the reason, there are definitely times when an instructional leader can learn from colleagues and other educators.

Challenge

- To be effective, an instructional leader must be willing to be open to the strategies and methods used by fellow instructional leaders.
- Instructional leaders need to help each other to improve just the same as teachers studying teaching together.

Plan

The basic steps for facilitating this single-focus seminar:

1. Provide time for a 60-minute seminar session with the leadership team and a follow-up session a week later.
2. Each leader selects one success story from those found on pages 181–207 and treats the success story as if it were his or her own. They are asked to think aloud about how the success story mirrors their instructional leadership practice.

3. One by one, each leader tells their story substituting some aspect of her or his own work that is similar to the one in the book.
4. When everyone has a chance to tell his or her story, the facilitator hands out "When Is Good Instructional Leadership Going On? copied from pages 207–209. The group uses this common ground (i.e., nine behaviors, actions, and practices for fostering exemplary instructional leadership) to reflect on their work.

Personal and Team Connections

- Participants will be asked to connect their unique leadership challenges to the content of the seminar.
- The team will ask two essential questions: (1) What have we been learning? (2) How can we use this learning to strengthen our work as instructional leaders?

FINAL REFLECTION

Yes, closing the teaching gap is an extraordinary challenge, but when looked at from the perspective of the dynamics of change, it does not have to take years and years. For example, think of how quickly the country has adjusted to the need to be better prepared against terrorism and how to survive in a global economy. *What is needed in education is a change in understanding.*

At the writing of this book, there are hopeful signs that a change in understanding might be right around the corner. Stronger, more united voices, are calling for a complete transformation from an educational system designed around 19th-century industrial practices to a new model of student-centered learning. Using an analogy similar to the thinking put forth by Lester Brown (2011) to prevent environmental and economic collapse, "Saving our education system is not a spectator sport."

As a final reflection, think of how your work as an instructional leader has helped in some way to close the teaching gap that exists in your school or district. What did you learn from this experience that will help you to become a better instructional leader?

The motivation for all your hard work as an instructional leader is summed up best in the statement below. Keep it in mind the next time you hit a snag or feel like things are not going well.

> *"We owe the most to the classroom teachers and school administrators who are fighting every day for their students and for decency in education."*

> –Saving Our Schools, Goodman, Shannon, Goodman, & Rapoport, Editors, 2004 (Acknowledgments)

Answers to In-Your-Head Quizzes

In-Your-Head Quiz #2: Best response is #3—In order to improve teaching, the teachers and I must treat teaching like an object of study.

In-Your-Head Quiz #3: Best response is #3—Teachers are working hard but not teaching for meaning and learning.

In-Your-Head Quiz #4: Because teaching is learned through informal participation over long periods. Teaching is something you learn to do more by growing up in a culture than by studying it formally. Everyone goes to school, so everyone learns what teaching is.

In-Your-Head Quiz #5: Professional development and in-service workshops.

In-Your-Head Quiz #6: #2: Communication with staff.

In- Your-Head Quiz #7: #2: Learning in the classroom.

In- Your-Head Quiz #8: School improvement.

In- Your-Head Quiz #9: 21st century, exists

References

Allen, D. (2001). *Getting things done.* London: Penguin Books.

Alvarado, A. (Speaker) (2005). [Video]. San Diego: San Diego Summer Leadership Institute.

Ambrose, S., Bridges, M., & DiPietro, M., Lovett, M., & Norman, M. (2010). *How learning works: Seven research-based principles for smart teaching.* San Francisco: Jossey-Bass.

Annenberg Institute for School Reform. (1997). *Looking at student work: A window into the classroom* [Video Package]. Providence, RI: AISR.

Argyris, C. (1991). Teaching smart people how to learn. *Harvard Business Review, 4,* 4–15.

Argyris, C., & Schön, D. (1978). *Organizational learning: a theory of action perspective.* Philippines: Addison-Wesley Publishing Company.

Barth, R. (February 2001). Teacher leader. *Phi Delta Kappan, 82,* 443–449.

Bill & Melinda Gates Foundation. (2010). *Learning about teaching: Initial findings from the measures of effective teaching project.* Retrieved from http://www.gatesfoundation.org/college-ready-education/Documents/preliminary-finding-policy-brief.pdf.

Blasé, J., & Blasé, J. (2004). *Handbook of instructional leadership* (2nd ed.). Thousand Oaks, CA: Corwin.

Bliss, E. (1980). *Getting things done.* New York: Bantam Books.

Brown, L. (2011). *World on the edge: How to prevent environmental and economic collapse.* W. W. Norton & Company.

Bruner, J. (1996). *The culture of education.* Cambridge, MA: Harvard University Press.

Cohen, W. (2010, September 1). *Three principles to developing yourself as a leader.* Retrieved from http://www.humanresourcesiq.com.

Curtis, R., & Wurtzel, J. (2010). *Teaching talent: A visionary framework for human capital in education.* Cambridge, MA: Harvard Education Press.

Danielson, C., (2006). *Teacher leadership that strengthens professional practice.* Alexandria, VA: Association for Supervision and Curriculum Development.

Danielson, C. (2007, September). The many faces of leadership. *Educational Leadership, 65*(1). Retrieved from http://www.ascd.org/publications/educational-leadership/sept07/vol65/num01/The-Many-Faces-of-Leadership.aspx.

Dewey, J. (1938). *Experience and education.* New York: Collier MacMillan Publishers.

Dewey, J. (1965). The relation of theory to practice in education. In M. Borrowman (Ed.), *Teacher education in America: A documentary history* (pp. 140–171). New York: Teachers College Press. (Original work published 1904)

Drucker, P. (1999, March). Managing oneself. *Harvard Business Review.*

Drucker, P. (2006). *The effective executive in action.* New York: Collins.

DuFour, R. (2004, May). Schools as learning communities. *Educational Leadership, 61,* 6–11.

Elmore, R., Peterson, P., & McCarthey, S. (1996). *Restructuring in the classroom: Teaching, learning, and school organization.* San Francisco: Jossey-Bass.

Evans, R. (2001). *The human side of change: Reform resistance, and the real-life problems of innovation.* San Francisco: Jossey-Bass.

Fenton, B. (2011). New *leaders for new schools: Forming aligned instructional leadership teams.* Retrieved from http://www.ascd.org/ascd-express/vol5/504-fenton.aspx.

Gallimore, R., & Ermeling, B. (2010, April 14). *Five keys to effective teacher learning teams. Education Week.* Retrieved from http://www.edweek.org/ew/articles/2010/04/13/29gallimore.h29.html.

Gallimore, R., Ermeling, B., Saunders, W., & Goldenberg, C. (2009). Moving the learning of teaching closer to practice: Teacher education implications of school-based inquiry teams. *The Elementary School Journal, 109,* 1–18.

Glickman, C. (2002). *Leadership for learning: How to help teachers succeed.* Alexandria, VA: Association for Supervision and Curriculum Development.

Goodman, K., Shannon, P., Goodman, Y., & Rapoport, R., Editors. (2004). Saving our schools: The case for public education, Saying no to "no child left behind." Berkeley, RDR Books.

Goslin, K. (2010, December 1). *Instructional leadership for the 21st century: Changes in teaching and schooling.* Presented at University of Prince Edward Island Institute, Prince Edward Island, Canada.

Guba, E., & Lincoln, Y. (1981). *Effective evaluation.* San Francisco: Jossey-Bass.

Haberman, M. (1991). The pedagogy of poverty versus good teaching. *Kappan, 73,* 90–294.

Hargreaves, A. (1994*). Changing teachers, changing times.* London: Caswell.

Harris, H. (2002). *School improvement: What's in it for schools*. New York: RoutledgeFalmer.

Harris Interactive. (2009). *MetLife survey of the American teacher.* New York: Author.

Harvard Change Leadership Group. (2006, April 15–16). *Three-day learning lab: Systemic change for student success.* Cambridge, MA: Harvard Graduate School of Education.

Hesselbein, F. (1999, Spring). The key to cultural transformation. *Leader to Leader Journal, 12*, 1–7.

Hiebert, J., Gallimore, R., & Stigler, J. (2002, June/July). A knowledge base for the teaching profession: What would it look like and how can we get one. *Educational Researcher, 31*, 3–15.

Johnson, W. (2008, May 27). *Successfully leading change*. Malvern, PA: Progressive Business Conference. Retrieved from https://www .pbconferences.com/audio/main.asp?G=2&E=1390&I=1.

Kelley, C. (2010, June). *High school leadership teams*. Madison: University of Wisconsin-Madison for the Wisconsin Urban School Leadership Project.

Knight, J. (2007). *Instructional coaching: A partnership approach to improving instruction.* Thousand Oaks, CA: Corwin.

Knight, J. (2009, March). What can we do about teacher resistance? *Kappan, 90*, 508–513.

Kohn, A. (2010, August 25). Turning children into data. *Education Week, 32*, 29.

Lambert L. (1998). *Building leadership capacity in schools.* Alexandria, VA: Association for Supervision and Curriculum Development.

Lambert, L. (2002). A framework for shared leadership. *Educational Leadership, 59*(8), 37–40.

Leithwood, K., Seashore Lewis, K., Anderson, S., & Wahlstrom, K. (2004). *Review of research: How leadership influences student learning.* New York: Learning from Leadership Project, The Wallace Foundation.

Leonard, L., & Leonard, P. (2002). Schools as professional communities: Addressing the collaborative challenge. *International Electronic Journal of Leadership in Learning, 7*(1).

Leonhirth, J. (2010, July 21). Communication mired in modern paradox. *The Daily News Journal*, p. 1.

Lesson Study Research Group. (2010). *Facts about lesson study*. Retrieved from http://www.tc.edu/lessonstudy/lessonstudy.html.

Lewis, C. (2000). *Lesson study: A handbook of teacher-led instructional change*. Philadelphia, PA: Research for Better Schools.

Lockhart, P. (2009). *Mathematician's lament*. New York: Bellevue Literary Press.

Marzano, R. (2009, October 30). *Supervising the art and science of teaching*. Presented at ASCD Fall Conference, Alexandria, VA.

McDonald, J., Mohr, N., Dichter, A., & McDonald, E. (2003). *The power of protocols: An educator's guide to better practice.* New York: Teachers College Press.

National Comprehensive Center for Teacher Quality. (2007). *Lessons learned: New teachers talk about their jobs, challenges, and long-range plans.* Washington, DC: Author.

National Institute of Child Health and Human Development Early Child Care Research Network. (2005). A day in the third grade: A large-scale study of classroom quality and teacher and student behavior. *Elementary School Journal, 105,* 305–323.

National Research Council. (2005). *How students learn* (S. Donovan & J. Bransford, Eds.). Washington, DC: The National Academic Press.

Oncken, William, Jr., & Wass, Donald, L. (1999, November/December). Management time: Who's got the monkeys? *Harvard Business Review,* 1–6.

Organization for Economic Co-operation and Development (OECD). (2011). *Strong performers and successful reformers in education: Lessons from the Program for International Student Assessment (PISA) for the United States.* OECD Publishing. Retrieved from http://dx.doi.org/10.1787/9789264096660-en.

Ravitch, D. (2010). *The death and life of the great American school system.* New York: Basic Books.

Riddile, M. (2010, December 15). *PISA: Poverty not stupid.* Retrieved from http://nasspblogs.org/principaldifference/2010/12/pisa_its_poverty_not_stupid_1.html.

Saunders, W., Goldenberg, C., & Gallimore, R. (2009). Increasing achievement by focusing grade-level teams on improving classroom learning: A prospective, quasi-experimental study of title schools. *American Educational Research Journal, 20,* 1–28.

Schön, D. (1983). *The reflective practitioner: How professionals think in action.* New York: Basic Books.

Seashore Lewis, K., & Wahlstrom, K. (2011, February). Principals as cultural leaders: Principals shape the culture in positive ways when they share leadership and take responsibility for shaping classroom improvements. *Kappan, 92*(5), 52–56.

Semadeni, J. (2010, May). When teachers drive their learning. *Educational Leadership, 67,* 68–69.

Stigler, J. (2010, June 9). Rethinking teacher accountability—before it's too late. *Education Week, 29*(33), 35.

Stigler, J., & Hiebert, J. (1999). *The teaching gap: Best ideas from the world's teachers for improving education in the classroom.* New York: Free Press.

Stigler, J., & Hiebert, J. (2009). *The teaching gap: Best ideas from the world's teachers for improving education in the classroom* (2nd ed.). New York: Free Press.

Stigler, J., & Hiebert, J. (2009, November). Closing the teaching gap. *Kappan, 91,* 32–37.

Stigler, J., & Thompson, B (2009, May). Thoughts on creating, accumulating, and utilizing shareable knowledge to improve teaching. *The Elementary School Journal, 109,* 1–16.

Takahashi, A. (2000). A current trends and issues in lesson study in Japan and the United States. *Journal of Japan Society of Mathematical Education, 82,* 15–21.

Takahashi, A., & Yoshida, M. (2004). Ideas for establishing lesson-study communities. *Teaching Children Mathematics, 10,* 436–443.

Tucker, M. (2010, March). An assessment system for the United States: Why not build on the best? National Center on Education and the Economy, at the National Conference on Next Generation K–12 Assessment Systems. Retrieved from http://www.k12center.org/publications.html.

U.S. Department of Education. (2009). *President Obama, U.S. Secretary of Education Duncan announce national competition to advance school reform* [Press release]. Retrieved from http://ed.gov/news/press releases/2009/07/07242009.html.

University of Wisconsin-Madison Teaching Academy. (2008). *Teaching circles.* Retrieved from https://tle.wisc.edu/teaching-academy/peer/tcircles.

van Gogh, V. (1887). *To Emile Bernard. Paris, about December 1887.* New York: Thaw Collection, The Morgan Library & Museum. Retrieved from http://vangoghletters.org/vg/letters/let575/letter.html.

Wagner, T. (2004). *How to use the 7 disciplines for strengthening instruction diagnostic.* President and Fellows of Harvard College, Harvard Change Leadership Group. Cambridge, MA: Harvard Change Leadership Group.

Wagner, T. (2003, November 12). Beyond testing: The 7 disciplines for strengthening instruction. *Education Week, 23,* 28, 30.

Wagner, T. (2008). *The global achievement gap.* New York: Basic Books.

Wagner, T., Kegan, R., Lahey, L., Lemons, R., Garnier, J., Helsing, D., Howell, A., & Rasmussen, H. (2006). *Change leadership: A practical guide to transforming our schools.* San Francisco: Jossey-Bass.

Waters, T., Marzano, R., & McNulty, B. (2003). *Balanced leadership: What 30 years of research tells us about the effect of leadership on student achievement.* Aurora, CO: Mid-continent Research for Education and Learning.

Wellman, B., & Lipton, L. (2004). *Data-driven dialogue: A facilitator's guide to collaborative inquiry.* Sherman, CT: MiraVia.

Wiggins, G., & McTighe, J. (2007). *Schooling by design: Mission, action, and achievement.* Alexandria, VA: Association for Supervision and Curriculum.

Wisconsin Department of Public Education. (2010, June). *Advancing student learning through distributed instructional leadership: A toolkit for high school leadership teams.* Retrieved from http://dpi.wi.gov/sprntdnt/pdf/distributed_leadership_toolkit.pdf.

York-Barr, J., & Duke, K. (2004). What do we know about teacher leadership? Findings from two decades of scholarship. *Review of Educational Research, 74*(3), 255–316.

Recommended Books and Publications

Below are the prime resources that have affected my understanding of teaching and learning as well as instructional leadership development the most. These individuals and organizations helped me grasp the "why" behind the "how" (form of triangulation with experience, research, and expert opinion) and influenced my work as a practitioner. Each citation has a summarizing note that connects the source with instructional leadership.

- *Experience and Education* by John Dewey, 1938.

A classic little book. Provides a perspective for traditional and progressive education. If you understand Dewey, you understand why we need to improve the way students learn. Dewey laid out the principles for interpreting experience in its educational functions and forces.

- *The Thread That Runs So True: A Mountain School Teacher Tells His Story* by Jesse Stuart, 1958.

The "thread that runs so true" is fun. Children learn by playing. Stuart worked in a Kentucky mountain school as a teacher, principal, and superintendent. He learned by experience that teaching is the greatest profession there is.

- *The Mind in Society: The Development of Higher Psychological Processes* by L. S. Vygotsky, 1978.

Vygotsky was a Russian Jew who got into the University of Moscow by lottery. He was a genius. Vygotsky's theory of development (i.e., Zone of Proximal Development—ZPD) is the basis for understanding the gradual release of responsibility and scaffolding learning. Teaching involves the act of identifying what a child knows and can do within the ZPD and then providing the appropriate scaffolding. You cannot understand developmental learning without understanding Vygotsky.

- *Organizational Learning: A Theory of Action Perspective* by Chris Argyris and Donald Schön, 1978.

Argyris and Schön provide a framework for how organizations learn or fail to learn. The authors believe that individual theories of action contribute to the learning systems they describe as "single-loop learning" and "double-loop learning." The book helps instructional leaders understand the basis for theories of action.

- *Getting Things Done* by Edwin Bliss, 1980.

I met Edwin Bliss at a workshop in 1974. I was a young principal. It was the first time I heard someone talk about time management. He asked everyone to list his or her top five goals. No one listed good health. His time-management strategies start by keeping a time log over a 2-week period. This book (there is a newer edition) will help instructional leaders who is concerned about the way they use their time.

- *The Reflective Practitioner: How Professionals Think in Action* by Donald Schön, 1983.

Another classic. You probably had to read it when you went through graduate school. Schön laid the foundation for becoming a reflective practitioner through what he called "reflection-in-action." He provided the rationale for using your work as a source of self-improvement. This book bridges the leadership gap between theory and practice.

- *The Whole Story: Natural Learning and the Acquisition of Literacy in the Classroom* by Brian Cambourne, 1988.

Unless you are into literacy development, you probably have never heard of this book. You want this book because Cambourne's extensive research with language development produced the

7 Conditions for Learning (Immersion, Demonstration, Expectation, Responsibility, Use, Approximation, and Response). These conditions provide the *lenses* for looking into classrooms.

- *We Learned From Each Other: A Teacher's Memoir* by Emma Osborne, 2001.

Emma was a great teacher. She began her career teaching in a one-room schoolhouse. She wrote this memoir when she was 91. This book is an inspiration for any educator. Here philosophy can be summed up as follows: "Guide each child toward a goal which is within his reach" (that is Vygotsky). "Let learning be a challenging and desirable adventure" (that is Dewey).

- *Developing Instructional Leaders* by Larry Lashway, 2002.

Lashway provides perhaps the best overview of the development of instructional leadership. He details how instructional leadership is defined and should be developed. It is interesting to see how instructional leadership has developed since Lashway wrote this piece in 2002. He was definitely on track.

- *Leadership for Learning: How to Help Teachers Succeed* by Carl Glickman, 2002.

A principal's principal. His Instructional Leadership Beliefs Inventory is an excellent self-assessment tool. You definitely should complete it. Glickman's idea of an instructional leader is someone who is in classrooms all the time and knows what he is doing when he is in there.

- *Balanced Leadership: What 30 Years of Research Tells Us About the Effect of Leadership on Student Achievement* by Tim Waters, Robert Marzano, Brian McNulty, Mid-continent Research for Education and Learning (McREL), 2003.

The McREL meta-analysis research revealed that leadership matters. A significant, positive correlation exists between effective school leadership and student achievement. McREL research identified 21 key leadership responsibilities, of which seven responsibilities are positively associated with change perceived to be second order.

- *How Leadership Influences Student Learning* by Keith Leithwood, Karen Seashore Lewis, Stephen Anderson, & Kyla Wahlstrom, 2004.

This research answers the question: Does effective education leadership make a difference in improving learning? The answer is "yes." This research shows that instructional leadership not only matters; it is second only to teaching among school-related factors in its impact on student learning.

- *How Students Learn,* National Research Council, 2005.

Based on the book *How People Learn,* the findings from this research established three principles of learning so important that every teacher and instructional leader must understand them: (1) teachers must engage students' preconceptions, (2) teachers must help students learn with understanding (facts and ideas in the context of a conceptual framework), and (3) teachers must help students become independent learners (metacognitive approach).

- *The Effective Executive in Action* by Peter Drucker, 2006.

Drucker spent his entire life studying organizations and leadership. He coined the phrase "knowledge worker." Drucker contends that effectiveness can be learned. His chapters on "Know Thy Time" and "Making Strength Productive" are a must-read for any instructional leader.

- *Change Leadership: A Practical Guide to Transforming Our Schools* by Tony Wagner, Robert Kegan, Lisa Laskow Lahey, Richard W. Lemons, Jude Garnier, Deborah Helsing, Annie Howell, and Harriette Thurber Rasmussen, 2006.

The authors head up the Harvard Change Leadership Group dedicated to helping education leaders improve their schools. The book drives change leadership. Wagner and Kegan provide a framework and protocols for collaborative inquiry around school improvement. Their vision of success is right on.

- *Instructional Coaching: A Partnership Approach to Improving Instruction* by Jim Knight, 2007.

This is the frontrunner of books on instructional coaching. Building on years of research at the University of Kansas Coaching project (http://www.instructionalcoach.org/), Jim Knight introduces the concept of "partnership philosophy" as one possible theoretical framework for instructional coaching. The foundation of this philosophy rests on seven principles (equality, choice, voice, dialogue, reflection, praxis, and reciprocity). This book is must reading for any instructional coach.

- *The Teaching ·Gap: Best Ideas from the World's Teachers for Improving Education in the Classroom* by James Steigler and James Hiebert, 2009.

By far, the best research on improving teaching. Be sure to read their six principles for gradual improvement: #1: Improvement is gradual and incremental; #2: Keep a constant focus on student learning goals; #3: Focus on teaching, not teachers; #4: Make improvements in context; #5: Make improvement the work of teachers; and #6: Build a system that can learn from its own experience.

- *Instructional Rounds in Education, A Network Approach to Improving Teaching and Learning* by Elizabeth City, Richard Elmore, Sarah Fiarman, and Lee Teitel, 2009.

Elmore and associates apply the medical model of "rounds" to "instructional rounds" as the process for translating knowledge systematically into practice. The research is anchored in theories of action using protocols for conducting instructional rounds. This is not to be confused with Classroom Walkthroughs.

- *Organizing Schools for Improvement: Lessons from Chicago* by Anthony Bryk et al., 2010.

Extensive long-term study of school improvement efforts in Chicago over a 7-year period. Bryk and associates identified a set of practices and conditions that were keys to improvement. One of their major findings was that "strong leadership" in the sense that principals are "strategic, focused on instruction."

- *The Death and Life of the Great American School System: How Testing and Choice Are Undermining Education* by Diane Ravitch, 2010.

Diane Ravitch has written a book critical of objectives of the U.S. Department of Education. She points out the problems with No Child Left Behind (NCLB), school choice, charter schools, Race to the Top, and closing community schools. Ravitch believes we need long-term planning to rebuild the system of education, better assessments, a coherent curriculum, and a different language of accountability.

- *How Learning Works: 7 Research-Based Principles for Smart Teaching* by Susan Ambrose, Michael W. Bridges, Michele DiPietro, Marsha C. Lovett, and Marie K. Norman, 2010.

This is a must-read for any instructional leader who wishes to bridge learning research and teaching practice. The 7 Principles in the form of questions are: (1) How does students' prior knowledge affect their learning? (2) How does the way students organize knowledge affect their learning? (3) What factors motivate students to learn? (4) How do students develop mastery? (5) What kinds of practice and feedback enhance learning? (6) Why do student development and course climate matter for student learning? (7) How do students become self-directed learners?

Index

CORWIN
A SAGE Company

The Corwin logo—a raven striding across an open book—represents the union of courage and learning. Corwin is committed to improving education for all learners by publishing books and other professional development resources for those serving the field of PreK–12 education. By providing practical, hands-on materials, Corwin continues to carry out the promise of its motto: **"Helping Educators Do Their Work Better."**